# HOW GREEN IS YOUR GARDEN?

## A guide to choosing environmentally safe products

### NICK BRANWELL

Foreword by Geoff Hamilton

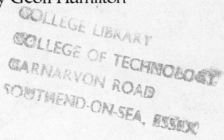

THORSONS

Thorsons Publishing Group

First published 1990


Copyright © Nick Branwell 1990

British Library Cataloguing in Publication Data
Branwell, Nick
How green is your garden? : a guide to choosing
environmentally safe products.
1: Gardens. Organic cultivation
635.0484


ISBN 0-7225-2144-8

*Published by Thorsons Publishers Limited, Wellingborough,
Northamptonshire NN8 2RQ, England*

Printed in Great Britain by Woolnough Bookbinding Limited,
Irthlingborough, Northamptonshire.
Typesetting by MJL Limited, Hitchin, Hertfordshire.


1 3 5 7 9 10 8 6 4 2

Special thanks to the Henry Doubleday Research Association
(HDRA) for attracting and sustaining my interest in organic
gardening, to Dr Andrew Slater for a different perspective, and
above all to Edwina Conner for encouraging me to write this book,
and for assistance of every kind.


Thanks are due to the following authors, copyright owners and publishers, for permission
to reprint extracts and illustrations from the following publications:

*Bouvard and Pecuchet* by Gustave Flaubert, translated by A.J. Krailsheimer (1976).
Reproduced by permission of Penguin Books Ltd.

*The Innocent Anthropologist* by Nigel Barley (1983). Reproduced by permission of British
Museum Publications Ltd.

*The Periodic Table* by Primo Levi, translated by Raymond Rosenthal (1984). Reproduced
by permission of Michael Joseph Ltd.

*Pest Control and its Ecology* by H.F. van Emden (1974). Reproduced by permission of
Edward Arnold.

*Vegetable Gardening* by Professor John Carey, from *The Sunday Times* 24th February
1980. Reproduced by permission of the author and Times Newspapers Ltd.

*The Gardener's Year* by Karel Capek (1931). Reproduced by kind permission of Unwin
Hyman Ltd.

*The Ages of Gaia* by James Lovelock (1988). Reproduced by permission of Oxford
University Press.

*Plant Pests and their Control* by P.G. Fenemore (1982). Illustration reproduced by
permission of Butterworth and Co (Publishers) Ltd.

*Henry Doubleday Research Association Newsletter 115* (1989). Illustration reproduced
by permission of H.D.R.A.

# Contents

# *Foreword*

For years organic gardening was seen as the sole preserve of the crank. The stereotype wore a scruffy beard, slopped about in kaftan and sandals and preached the joys of living 'close to the soil' from a terraced house in Paddington. Now that's all changed.

'Green' is the buzzword of the nineties. Quite suddenly, the world has woken up to the horrors we're creating for ourselves, and good men and women everywhere vie with each other to be greener than green. It's sometimes difficult for people who have been patiently working for years to generate an understanding and sympathy with those issues not to be cynical.

But this new enthusiasm *must* be welcomed and encouraged. It's a small start, but a start it certainly is. We all have a responsibility to build on it and to try to increase awareness and, above all, understanding. What we must avoid at all costs is allowing our enthusiasm to run away with us in the absence of that understanding.

Most of us remember the great 'hippie' revolution of the sixties and early seventies. For me, they were heady days. Certainly the long hair, the beads and blankets and the fact that everyone was 'Man', regardless of sex, took a bit of getting used to. But at least these

young folk gave you flowers instead of abuse. There can't be a lot wrong with that.

It became fashionable too, to grow things, (especially if you could smoke it!) Filled with determination and idealism, dozens of young people clubbed together to buy a bit of rock in Wales with the intention of becoming 'self-sufficient'. Many formed together into large communes to escape the rat-race and what they saw as the prison of modern civilized life. Alas, few remain.

They failed in the main, not because their idealism was flawed and not because they couldn't take the tough and uncomfortable life. They simply didn't have the practical knowledge and experience to prise a living from their reluctant soil.

I well remember how the dangers were brought home to me. I was the editor of a gardening magazine at the time, and one day I received a phone call. The chap on the other end intended to 'go self-sufficient.' He was leaving his job and had bought a house with a large area of land. Could I recommend a suitable rotovator for his needs?

Naturally, I first needed to know how big the piece of land was. From then on, I was fortunately able to persuade him that the last thing he should do was to give up his job because it just wasn't possible to become self-sufficient on three-quarters of an acre!

I was running a highly successful series of articles on self-sufficiency at the time, so you can imagine my horror. How many other people had we persuaded to risk all up certain failure? My next editorial issued severe warnings of bankruptcy, poverty and misery unless you knew what you were about.

Now we have a second opportunity to persuade large numbers of people into a more natural, gentler way of life and we simply can't afford to fail this time. And what better way to familiarize yourself with nature's ways than in your own back yard? There's no risk, no strife, no tearing up of roots and starting again. All that's needed is a change of emphasis.

I've been gardening organically now for more than twelve years and, to my joy, I discover that, not only does it work, it works *better* than the chemical methods we have copied from the farmer and commercial grower. My garden has never looked so green and healthy, it has never seen so many birds, bees and butterflies and my fruit and vegetables have never tasted so good.

But let's not make the same mistake we made in the seventies. The *only* way to be successful organically is to know what you're doing and to have a good understanding of why you're doing it. That's why I welcome this book.

There are plenty of 'organic' books available now, which are filled with a rich mixture of good gardening, folk-lore and old-wives tales. It's often hard to sort the wheat from the chaff.

*How Green is Your Garden?* sets out to give you that necessary basic understanding. When you've read it, you'll know not just *how* to do things, but *why*.

Geoff Hamilton

# Introduction

This book is about what we put on our gardens: fertilizers and manures and soil conditioners to make plants grow, weedkillers or herbicides to stop plants growing, and those other '-cides' which kill fungi, insects, mites, slugs, eelworms, earthworms, mice and many more. All these come under the heading of pesticides. The book is not about how to solve specific problems in the garden but about why some types of fertilizer or pesticide are considered more beneficial or harmful than others.

'Organic' gardening has been with us for many years, but has recently increased enormously in popularity. In most people's minds this means not using 'chemicals'. In this book we will look into the meaning of 'organic' and also see what these 'chemicals' are.

There are many different types and sizes of garden. At one extreme there may be a town patio, perhaps 4 metres by 2, covered with paving slabs or concrete, with a few potted plants on it. At the other extreme are gardens so large as to be effectively small farms, producing vegetables on an economic scale. The patio gardener will be more interested in the different types of commercially produced compost to fill tubs rather than in ways of making compost, or in different types of animal manure. The owner of a small orchard will have many more difficult decisions to make about pesticide use. But a street full of patio gardens might occupy a similar area to a smallholding, so they add up to the same amount of environment.

Gardeners are not farmers, they do not have to make a profit to survive, their labour is free. They don't have to do anything at all in the garden — if they prefer they can let it run to weeds. On the other hand, even if useful amounts of crops are produced, it won't affect the bank balance if the carrot crop fails. With cheap and varied vegetables available everywhere, even organic ones, fewer gardeners bother with growing vegetables than in the past, and more go for purely ornamental gardens.

Gardeners do not have to put anything on their gardens — no fertilizers, no pesticides, no compost — and many garden plants may thrive even then. But most plants grow much better if we give them some preferential treatment: this involves fertilizer of one kind or another, and some kind of pest control, chemical or otherwise. This book will try to help you find your way through the maze of products and advice. The word 'green' has now entered most people's vocabulary and many are either green or wish to be seen to be green — including politicians and business people. The word 'green' means 'naive', 'innocent', and 'inexpert', as well as 'environmentally sound'. Hopefully, this book will take some of the first meaning out of your environmental greenness.

Let us consider the average gardener, who has a garden of, say, 15 metres by 10, and wants to grow some flowers, shrubs and small trees, a patch of lawn, and perhaps a few vegetables and some fruit. This gardener's house may be in the middle of a terrace in which case farmyard manure cannot be delivered without messing up the hall carpet. There is a small compost heap in the garden but tea leaves and cabbage leaves plus a few lawn mowings don't seem to make very much compost, and someone keeps putting rose prunings on it. Recently many gardeners have developed a 'Green Conscience' and when it comes to dealing with slugs on the lettuces and hostas, greenfly or mildew on the roses, and convolvulus and ground elder which keep creeping under the fence, they may: use no chemicals at all to deal with them; use a chemical but feel guilty and furtive about it; or use some preparation marketed as being 'safe', 'organic' or 'natural'. As 'organic' gardening becomes more popular, more 'organic' products become available, and a trip to the garden centre exposes the innocent (green) to another, sometimes confusing, area of marketing.

'Organic' products come in similar packages to the others and are comparable in cost. What's the difference?

Since a fair amount of the book is about 'chemicals', part of the first chapter attempts to explain some basic chemistry. To any reader with a reasonable knowledge of chemistry, it will seem quite inadequate and over-simplified; to some other readers it may seem like doubledutch; but with luck the rest will find it useful. There is also a certain amount of what might be called soil science, and biology. The intention is not to baffle the reader but to give some idea of what goes on in soil and plants, since these processes are affected by the use of fertilizers and pesticides.

Finally, there is a glossary of terms, and tables giving details of hundreds of garden products to help you assess their 'green-ness'.

# 1
# *Everything is chemical*

What we put on our gardens includes: fertilizers, manures, composts and pesticides. They will all be dealt with at greater length, but what follows serves as an introduction.

*Fertilizers* have nothing to do with 'fertility' in any sexual sense. If you transfer pollen from the male part of a flower to the female part, you are fertilizing it and the plant will set seed. Fertilizers provide plants with the nutrients they need to grow properly. Manures are fertilizers too, but normally 'manure' implies something bulky, maybe smelly, such as farmyard manure — a mixture of cow dung and straw. Also 'compost', the result of rotting down vegetable waste, is a kind of manure.

Fertilizers generally mean something out of a packet that has been made in a factory, chemical and concentrated, like 'Growmore'. There are also 'organic' fertilizers such as dried blood or bonemeal. Fertilizers contain a mixture of chemicals which are necessary for plants to grow. So do manures, but in a less concentrated form and in less strictly controlled proportions. The three major components of a fertilizer are nitrogen, phosphorus and potassium (potash).

Nitrogen (N) is a gas which comprises 70 per cent of the atmosphere, but plants cannot get it in this form: it must be in the form of a soluble compound which can be taken in through roots or leaves. Combined with carbohydrate it forms protein which everyone has heard of.

Phosphorus (P) is commonly described as the element needed by the roots, but the matter is more complex than that. Certain phosphorus compounds can store and release large amounts of energy as required, rather like a battery, so phosphorus is required whenever the plant is actively growing and needs energy.

Potassium (K) is the third major element required. Gardeners often think of it as the element needed for flowers and fruit, but it may be the stems on which they grow that actually need it.

Other elements are necessary for plants to grow. They are just as important, but are required in smaller — sometimes tiny — quantities. These include sulphur, calcium, iron and others.

It must not be forgotten that the bulk of a plant comes from water and air. Carbon, hydrogen and oxygen make up the carbohydrates, such as sugar, which are then converted into the multitude of substances that make plant tissues. Water supplies hydrogen and oxygen, which can be 'added' along with fertilizers, but carbon can only come from carbon dioxide in the air, which is drawn in through the leaves.

Balanced fertilizers, such as 'Growmore', are a combination of nitrogen (N), phosphorus (P) and potassium (K) necessary for average requirements. Soil is rarely equally deficient in all three, and may be deficient in minor elements, so using this kind of product exclusively is bound to lead to problems eventually.

'Phostrogen' on the other hand contains more potassium than nitrogen or phosphorus, and also some minor elements, so it is sold as a 'complete' plant food. If you use a chemical fertilizer on pot plants or garden tubs, it is essential to use this kind of product as there is no soil to provide trace elements in the long term.

*Manures* contain the same ingredients as fertilizers but in unconcentrated form and with the proportions varying enormously. Fresh manure may contain a lot of nitrogen which may 'burn' the delicate roots of young plants if it is dug in shortly before sowing seed or transplanting, but this is just as true of chemical nitrogen fertilizers.

*Compost* means home-made garden compost. It is the subject of endless discussion and of many books, and there are many commercial and amateur designs for compost makers. Because it is basically decomposed vegetable matter, it is logical that it should form ideal plant food.

Compost also means the various mixtures of peat, sand and nutrients sold as 'seed', 'potting' or 'general purpose' compost. This is also known as 'soil-less' compost because it contains no soil, and it has largely superseded 'John Innes' compost which has the additional ingredient known as 'loam'. Loam, in this sense of the word, means, or is supposed to mean, rotted turf, but fre-

quently it was any old subsoil which merely added weight to the bag. There are also soil conditioners, green manures, mulches, peat, leaf mould and so on, all of which are discussed later.

*Pesticides* are anything that will kill, or adversely affect at least, any living thing you decide is a pest, including weeds.

Lilies of the valley are usually considered desirable plants, but when they take over the garden against your wishes they become a weed. Ground elder, one of the most tedious and invasive pests around, is reputed to have been introduced to this country by the Romans as a food plant. In a lawn, any plant other than grass is a weed; in most other garden situations it is the grass that is the weed. Different kinds of poison affect different kinds of plant in different ways — the categories of herbicides are discussed later. The dream is of a herbicide to kill only the weed and to harm nothing else. A well-known herbicide, paraquat, is probably equally well known as a poisoner of people.

Fungicides kill fungi, which include moulds, mildew and various organisms which don't look like mushrooms, such as the fungus that causes peach leaf curl. As forms of life, fungi are more closely related to plants than to animals, and one of the problems with fungicides is their tendency to damage plants.

Insecticides kill insects and many other types of small animal, such as mites and earthworms, and even higher forms of life, such as birds and mammals. Insecticides cause more controversy than other pesticides — partly because many of them are highly poisonous to animals, but perhaps more because of their general effect on the environment. Nearly all are poisonous to bees, for instance, which are the main pollinators of plants.

Molluscicides kill slugs and snails. They are usually used in the form of bait — small

14

pellets — and the active ingredients are also poisonous to birds and mammals. Recently, various 'safe' slug killers have been marketed, all containing aluminium sulphate — most definitely a 'chemical', but used by organic gardeners. The same chemical is used to acidify soil sufficiently to make hydrangeas grow blue flowers, and as a water purifier. In 1988 a large quantity of aluminium sulphate was dumped into the water supply in Camelford in Cornwall, causing acute and chronic problems to thousands of people. However, its efficacy as a slug killer seems a bit doubtful.

What else do we put on our gardens? Mixtures of the above: fertilizers with weedkillers, fungicides with insecticides, growth regulators, cat and dog repellants, wood preservatives.

All of these are *chemicals*. The word 'chemical' has acquired an aura of horror in recent years, not surprisingly with the number of disasters involving chemicals. Chemicals, to many people, are somehow inherently dangerous. Most people will have done some chemistry at school and will know that matter — the substance forming everything — is composed of *elements* and *compounds*. Water is $H_2O$ — two atoms of hydrogen with one of oxygen — and the symbol $H_2O$ represents one *molecule* of water. Water is a chemical. Sulphuric acid is $H_2SO_4$ — two atoms of hydrogen with one of sulphur and four of oxygen. It is also a chemical and seems more like one because it is dangerous. It was one of the first weedkillers. Sulphuric acid can be obtained by combining water ($H_2O$) with sulphur dioxide ($SO_2$), a gas emitted in large amounts by industry. When this happens in the atmosphere we get the infamous acid rain, but curiously, the sulphur in acid rain supplies plants with some of the sulphur they need.

When sulphuric acid is diluted in water it becomes two separate parts called *ions*, which are, equally and oppositely, electrically charged. Hydrogen ions are $H^+$ — positively charged *cations* — and sulphate ions, $SO_4^{--}$, have two negative charges and are *anions*. Since the opposite charges must balance each other, there are two $H^+$ for every one $SO_4^{--}$. So sulphuric acid is $H_2^+SO_4^{--}$.

Sodium hydroxide (caustic soda), which is used to strip paint from old pine furniture, is an *alkali* (or *base*), NaOH. Dissolved in water, it also separates into ions: $Na^+OH^-$. One of the experiments usually done in schools is adding caustic soda to hydrochloric acid ($H^+Cl^-$), to find at what point the acid neutralizes the base. $Na^+OH^- + H^+Cl^- \rightarrow Na^+Cl^- + H_2O$, or salt (sodium chloride), plus water. These three — acid, base and salt — are completely soluble substances. Other acids and bases are 'weaker' because they do not dissociate so much in water, and other 'salts' such as calcium carbonate (chalk) — $CaCO_3$ — are hardly soluble at all, but become more so if placed in acid solution. *Acidity* is measured on a scale called pH (technically the logarithmic measure of the number of $H^+$ ions in a solution), which goes from 0 to 14. Zero is very acid; 14 is very alkaline; 7 is neutral — like water. Plants and other organisms will grow in soils where the pH ranges from about 4 to 8.5. The acids and bases involved in living systems are far more complex than HCl and NaOH, but the overall acidity can be expressed as the excess or shortage of $H^+$ ions.

Most of the chemicals used as fertilizers are soluble ionic compounds. They are also *inorganic*. *Organic* originally means substances derived from living organisms, or chemically similar. The study of chemistry is divided into organic and inorganic chemistry.

**Inorganic chemicals** used by gardeners include:

HOW GREEN IS YOUR GARDEN?

| | | |
|---|---|---|
| Copper sulphate | $Cu^{++}SO_4^{--}$ | Fungicide |
| Mercurous chloride | $Hg^+Cl^-$ | Fungicide |
| Ammonium nitrate | $NH_4^+NO_3^-$ | Nitrogen fertilizer |
| Calcium carbonate | $Ca^{++}CO_3^{--}$ | Limestone, chalk |
| Potassium chloride | $K^+Cl^-$ | Potassium fertilizer |
| Triplesuperphosphate | $Ca^{++}(H_2PO_4^-)_2$ | Phosphate fertilizer |

Of these, mercurous chloride, or calomel, is poisonous to most forms of life. Copper sulphate, an *inorganic* chemical, is one of the few fungicides tolerated by *organic* gardeners.

What is an **organic chemical**? All organisms — living creatures — are made up of similar substances and they all contain carbon. Carbohydrates, like sugar and starch, are compounds of carbon, hydrogen and oxygen. Carbon is a 'special' element in that it can combine with itself and other elements or compounds in an astonishing number of ways. It can make chains and rings and structures of enormous complexity, and very slight differences in the arrangement of the components can completely change the properties of a compound. For chemists, an organic chemical is one with carbon in it. Oil, plastics, petrol and most pesticides are organic chemicals. Yet most of the chemicals to which 'organic' gardeners object are organic. It is essential to stress these obviously different uses of the word, and not to confuse them. This is difficult so, wherever it might be ambiguous, the garden type of organic will have quotation marks around it.

Organic molecules are best described by a drawing because of their complexity. For example, the notorious paraquat looks like Fig. 1.

Each hexagon has six carbon atoms, and the lines — double or single — joining them are molecular bonds. On either side of each 'ring' the hydrogen has been replaced with a nitrogen atom, to each of which is connected a 'methyl' group ($CH_3$). The plus sign by each N indicates that the whole thing is actually a *cation*. Because of this it sticks to soil particles which are negatively charged, and so it becomes 'soil inactivated', which conceals the fact that it is very stable and may take years to break down.

Another molecule with a bad reputation is 'gamma HCH', shown in Fig. 2.

This is also a ring of carbon atoms, where the normal hydrogen atoms on each point have been joined by a chlorine atom. In addition, what this two-dimensional picture cannot show is that the Hs and Cls may point up or down from the ring: there are in fact eight different versions (isomers) of HCH (hexachlorocyclohexane), of which only one — the 'gamma' isomer — is a useful insec-

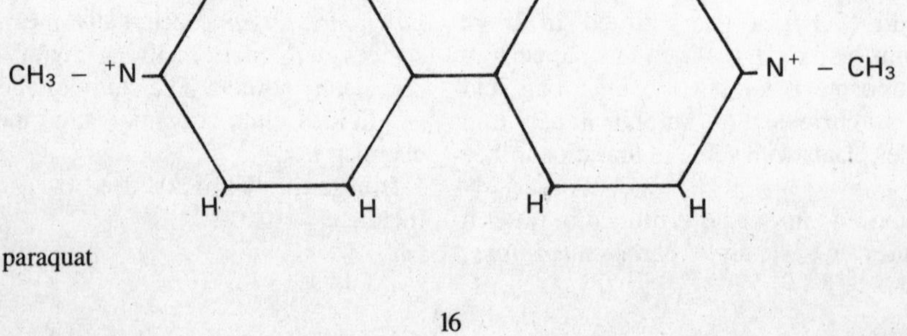

Fig 1: paraquat

16

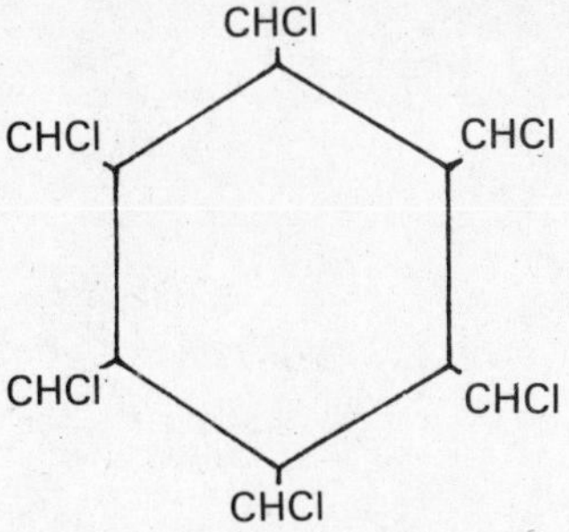

CHCl

CHCl          CHCl

CHCl          CHCl

CHCl

Fig 2: gamma HCH

ticide. Gamma HCH, like DDT and other 'organochlorines', is well known for its stability and persistence. However, this common phenomenon of the very close similarity between two organic substances — one toxic, the other not — is one of the mechanisms whereby pests acquire resistance to a pesticide: they manufacture enzymes which detoxify the poison by a simple chemical alteration.

Some of the pesticides considered 'safe' by 'organic' gardeners are organic chemicals: plant extracts such as derris and pyrethrum, which break down very quickly; but another, copper sulphate, is inorganic and about as persistent as they come.

It is important to stress that everything is chemical: we may or may not believe that living things are *more* than that but they are never *less* than that. So when we eat our 'organically' grown carrots, we are eating chemicals, albeit in a very complicated form (see Fig. 3). The most important difference between plants and animals is that plants must get their food in very simple forms: as inorganic chemicals, or *minerals*.

Plants cannot take in 'food' — such as manure — through their roots; they take in simple ions, either elemental, calcium ($Ca^{++}$), chlorine ($Cl^-$) or as simple ionic groups, like ammonium ($NH_4^+$), phosphate ($H_2PO_4^-$) or nitrate ($NO_3^-$), although they can take in certain organic molecules — see Chelates in the A to Z. It used to be thought until the last century that plants actually fed on humus, which is partially decomposed vegetable matter, full of nutrients, but chemically very complex. In fact, soil microorganisms have to break this down much further before those nutrients are available to the plant. The problem that we face now is that since it has been established that plants feed on chemicals, soil has been treated as a kind of 'nutrient bin', and a place for plants to anchor themselves, and not much more. Treating the soil as if it were dead is the best way to kill it, and in harsh climates soil can be destroyed in no time at all. Even in Britain it is happening, and in some areas much faster than most people realize.

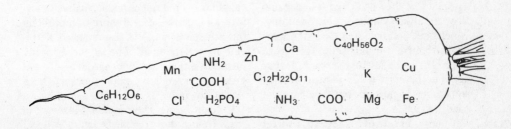

Fig 3: an organically grown carrot

# 2
# A little history

*F*arming and gardening methods vary all over the world and have constantly changed over the years. In the light of the amount of horticultural writing about today, and passionate insistence on particular methods over others, it is fascinating to see how writers have had their dogmas and disagreements in the past.

Jethro Tull (1674-1740) first proposed growing crops in rows, and insisted that regular ploughing obviated the need for any fertilizer. (In those days there was *only* 'organic' fertilizer.) William Cobbett, in *The English Gardener*, writes:

> Mr Tull very justly complained that those who condemned his scheme (and it is curious that Voltaire was one of these) and asserted that they had *tried* it and found it to fail, always omitted some one thing, which omission rendered the other operations abortive. Mr Tull said: 'Their great error is in the misuse of the word IT: they say they have tried IT: they have tried something, to be sure, but they have not tried my scheme.'
>
> Voltaire, in one of his letters (I forget to whom) says, as nearly as I can recollect the words, 'I have tried the famous system of Mr Tull of England, and I confess

to you that I find it to be abominable.' He goes on, however, to show most satisfactorily that it was not the system of Mr Tull that he had tried, for he says, 'the intervals, or the spaces, between the ridges were, from the month of May, full of weeds, which quickly smothered the wheat.' So he had tried it after the manner of those whom Mr Tull had complained of in England; that is to say, he had made the ridges, sowed the rows of wheat, all in very exact proportions as to distance and everything else; but he had not ploughed or horsehoed the intervals; whereas that operation was the very soul of the system.

Growing crops in rows has, of course, caught on — but not as an alternative to fertilizer — and weeds are more of a problem this way: farmers use large amounts of herbicide to get round it. One of the favourite methods among organic gardeners is *not* growing crops in rows, but in blocks, to keep weeds down!

Cobbett wrote *The English Gardener* in 1829. He uses the example of Jethro Tull and growing crops in rows as an example of the importance of *principles*. He goes on to describe various principles that might surprise the gardener of today. To the compost for about half an acre (10 by 15 rods) he recommended adding 'about thirty bushels of salt, perhaps that would be enough for the whole extent of the garden at one time'. To be fair, he was aware that adding too much would harm earthworms, and the plants themselves.

Another principle was to hoe the roots off vegetables. 'The roots, thus cut asunder, shoot again from the plant's side, find new food and send, instantly, fresh vigour to the plant.' He also insisted on transplanting in hot sun and into dry soil, rather than in damp weather and into moist soil. 'I would prefer no rain for a month, to rain at the time of planting.'

Cobbett was against watering plants in general: 'Watering plants, though so strongly recommended in English gardening books, and so much in practice, is a thing of very doubtful utility in any case, and, in most cases, of positive injury.'

Before going on to describe the cultivation of individual vegetables, Cobbett finished:

I shall conclude this chapter with observing, on what I deem a vulgar error, and an error which sometimes produces inconvenience. It is believed, and stated, that the ground grows tired, in time, of the same sort of plant, and that, if it be, year after year, cropped with the same sort of plant, the produce will be small, and the quality inferior to what it was at first.

Crop rotation is, of course, one of the foundation stones of organic gardening.

Cobbett's garden was nevertheless a success, perhaps for two reasons. His soil must have been wonderful — otherwise he could not have had it dug every year to the amazing depth of 3 feet 9 inches! Secondly, it is probable that his employees ignored his instructions! He says of gardeners, 'Every gardener thinks that everyone who employs him is, as far as relates to gardening, a natural born fool... They receive his directions very quietly, then go away and pay no more attention to them than to the whistling of the winds.'

Not all of Cobbett's principles sound as odd as those I have quoted, and much of what he wrote seems perfectly normal to the modern reader. But when it came to pest control he was as lost as anyone else:

I know nothing but fire or boiling water or squeezing to death that will destroy ants; and if you pour boiling water on their nests in the grass, you destroy the grass; set fire to a nest of the great ants, and you burn up the hedge or the trees, or whatever else is in the neighbourhood. As to squeezing them to death, they are among the twigs and roots of your trees and plants, they are in the blossoms and creeping all about the fruit, so that to destroy them in this way you must destroy that also which you wish to protect against their depredations.

Cobbett despairs of the 'Black grub', some kind of cutworm or leatherjacket.

This is a most perverse as well as a most pernicious thing; it is not content, like the caterpillar, the snail or the slug, to feed upon the leaves, but it must needs bite out the heart, or just cut off the plant at the bottom. Lime has no power over it: nothing will keep it off, no means but taking it by the hand.

Apart from quicklime on slugs, the only chemical mentioned is nicotine (tobacco smoke, tobacco water), which is effective against lice (aphids), bugs and maggots (sawfly).

In Flaubert's *Bouvard and Pécuchet* (1880) we see an early example of two middle-class office-workers trying to give up the city life, get it together in the country and go self-sufficient.

> They already saw themselves in shirt-sleeves, beside a flower bed, pruning roses, and digging, hoeing, handling the soil, transplanting things. They would awake to the sound of the lark and follow the plough, they would go with a basket to pick apples, they would watch butter-making, grain threshing, sheep shearing, bee-keeping and would revel in the low-ing of the cattle and the smell of the new mown hay. No more copying! No more boss! No more rent even! For they would own their own home! And they would eat chickens from their own poultry-run, vegetables from their own garden — and would sit down to dinner with their clogs on! We'll do whatever we please! We'll grow beards!

However, Bouvard and Pécuchet had no experience of what they were getting into, did everything wrong, and then tried to get their knowledge from books.

> They took each other's advice, opened one book, went over to another, then did not know what to decide when opinions diverged so widely. Thus, regarding marl, Purvis recommends it, Roret's manual opposes it. As for plaster [gypsum], despite Franklin's example, Rieffel and Monsieur Rigaud do not seem very keen. Fallows, according to Bouvard, were a Gothic prejudice. Yet Leclerc cites cases where they are indispensable. Gasparin quotes a Lyonnais farmer who for fifty years grew cereals in the same field: that disproves the theory of rotation of crops. Tull makes much of ploughing at the expense of fertilizer, and here is Major Beetson doing away with fertilizer and ploughing!

There follows a hilarious description of making compost, and the end result:

> Aroused by Pécuchet he went into a frenzy about fertilizer. In the compost pit were heaped up branches, blood, intes-tines, feathers, anything he could find. He used Belgian liqueur, Swiss 'lizier', wash-ing soda, smoked herrings, seaweed, rags, had guano sent, tried to make it — and carrying his principles to the limit, did not tolerate any waste of urine; he did away with the lavatories. Dead animals were brought into his yard, and used to fertilize his land. This disembowelled car-rion was strewn over the countryside. Bouvard smiled amid all this infection. A pump fixed up in a farm cart spread out liquid manure over the crops. If people looked disgusted he would say 'But it is gold! Gold!' And he was sorry not to have still more dungheaps. How fortunate are those countries with natural caves full of bird droppings! The colza was poor, the oats mediocre, the wheat could scarcely be sold on account of its smell. One odd thing was that the mound, finally cleared of its stones, was less productive than before.

Isaac Emerton gives two recipes for com-post in *The culture and management of the Auricula* (1815). Compost no. 2:

2 Barrowsful of goose dung, steeped in bul-locks blood
2 Barrowsful of sugar bakers scum
2 Barrowsful of night soil
2 Barrowsful of fine yellow loam

Karel Čapek in *The Gardener's Year* (1931) puts the whole business into perspective.

> Some people say that charcoal should be added, and others deny it; some recom-mend a dash of yellow sand, because it is supposed to contain iron, while others

warn you against it for the very fact that it does contain iron. Others, again, recommend clean river sand, others peat alone, and still others sawdust. In short, the preparation of the soil for seeds is a great mystery and a magic ritual. To it should be added marble dust (but where to get it?), three-year-old cow dung (but here it is not clear whether it should be the dung of a three-year-old cow or a three-year-old heap), a handful from a fresh molehill, clay pounded to dust from old pigskin boots, sand from the Elbe (but not from the Vitava), three-year-old hot-bed soil, and perhaps besides the humus from the golden fern and a handful from the grave of a hanged virgin — all that should be well mixed (gardening books do not say whether at the new moon, or full, or on midsummer night); and when you put this mysterious soil into flower pots (soaked in water, which for three years have been standing in the sun, and on whose bottoms you put pieces of boiled crockery, and a piece of charcoal, against the use of which other authorities, of course, express their opinions) — when

you have done all that, and so obeyed hundreds of prescriptions, principly contradicting each other, you may begin the real business of sowing the seeds.

One can sympathize with those people who welcomed the arrival of clean, odourless, chemical, balanced compound fertilizers, ready-made John Innes composts, each designed for a different purpose, and weedkillers and insecticides that released gardeners from so much labour and guesswork.

We can see that people have been arguing about the best way to do things for a long time; the debate continues; now there is a general polarization of opinion between 'organic' and 'conventional' methods. Many 'organic' gardeners are like Cobbett: you must follow the principles exactly. If anything goes wrong, it is because you must have deviated in some way from the principles.

Until quite recently there was only 'organic' farming and gardening. Let us trace the origins of what have now become 'conventional' methods.

# Fertilizers

Since the year dot, farmers have returned waste from crops, their animals, and themselves, back to the land. The Romans were aware of the value of 'marling' — adding lime and clay to the soil — and growing legumes (peas and beans) to fix extra nitrogen (though they did not realize what they were doing!)

This carried on until the nineteenth century, by which time scientists were aware of the major nutrients that plants required. Bones were imported to supply phosphorus, and sodium nitrate and guano (bird droppings) were brought from South America for nitrogen as well as phosphate. The Rotham-

sted Experimental Station was founded in 1840 by John Bennett Lawes who dissolved bones in sulphuric acid, and set up a superphosphate factory. The fertilizer industry had begun. Soon, ammonium sulphate was being manufactured as a by-product of coal. Deposits of potassium salts were discovered in France and Germany and mined from 1880 onwards. The 'Haber-Bosch' process was a new dimension: it fixed atmospheric nitrogen as ammonia ($NH_3$), and drew fertility from thin air. It was as big a leap as the discovery that legumes fixed nitrogen. All you needed was plenty of fossil fuel to provide the energy for the process. All manner of nitrogen fertilizers derive from the production of ammonia; recently liquid ammonia has been directly injected into the soil, without bothering to convert it to anything else first.

A fairly new development is slow-release nitrogen fertilizer. A particular advantage of this is that the release is slowest in cold weather — when plant growth is also slowest — and at maximum in warm weather when plants are growing most quickly. This reduces the much-publicized problem of nitrate leaching. Another solution to the leaching problem is to use ammonium fertilizers with a built-in 'nitrification inhibitor'. (See section on soil.)

The other fertilizer ingredients — phosphate and potassium — are still dependent on being dug out of the earth, and are available in their original state: 'rock phosphate' and 'rock potash', but for modern fertilizers they are converted into soluble salts. Potassium sulphate, potassium chloride and triple-superphosphate are the most common; but there are also 'compound' fertilizers which supply more than one main nutrient, such as potassium nitrate and ammonium phosphate. Fertilizers are normally sold as a mixture with nitrogen, phosphorus, and potassium in varying proportions, and in granulated form.

# Insecticides

A little biology textbook called *Pest Control and its Ecology* by J.F. van Emden begins:

> The history of modern pest control dates from the second half of the nineteenth century when the Colorado beetle spread rapidly across the USA and seriously threatened food production and the national economy. After much argument it was finally decided to take the unprecedented step of spraying the potato crops with a human poison (arsenic in the form of Paris Green). It would be inhuman to claim it as unfortunate that the prophesied human mass mortality did not occur, but there is no doubt that Colorado beetle control with Paris Green opened up the way to the use of biocides (destroyers of life in general) on crops destined for human consumption.

The point is that if masses of people had died, perhaps the 'poison' approach to pests would have been abandoned, and we would not be in the pickle we're in now. The early insecticides included arsenic compounds — obviously very poisonous to people — tar oils which, owing to their phytotoxicity (adverse affect on plants), could be used only on dormant trees, and poisonous plant extracts such as pyrethrum, derris and nicotine. Derris was used in Malaya traditionally as a fish poison, as a lazy way of catching fish. Evidently people have long been aware, in different parts of the world, that substances which are poisonous are even more so to fish. Nigel Barley, in *The Innocent Anthropologist* (1983), describes a semi-primitive tribe in Cameroon.

> As far as 'living in harmony with nature' is concerned, the Dowayos are non-starters... When Dowayos began cultivating cotton for the government monopoly, amounts of pesticide were made available to them. Dowayos immediately adopted it for fishing purposes. They would fling it into the streams to be able to recover the poisoned fish that floated to the surface. This poison rapidly replaced the tree-bark they had traditionally used to suffocate fish. 'It's wonderful,' they explained, 'You throw it in and it kills everything — small fish, big fish, for miles downstream'.

Modern insecticides began with the organochlorines in the 1930s. DDT was the first and most famous. When first invented, DDT seemed like a perfect solution: it lasted a long time and so did not have to be constantly reapplied; it worked by contact, ingestion and even by vapour action; was effective for a wide range of pests and was much less poisonous to humans or livestock than, for example, arsenic. Its use really took off during the Second World War. Lice spread typhus. There was an epidemic of typhus in Naples in 1943, and the civilian population of the town was treated with DDT to prevent the spread of typhus to the invading army. DDT-impregnated shirts were standard issue to British troops going to the Continent.

Another reason for the rapid rise of DDT was that derris and pyrethrum were unavailable: the Japanese were major suppliers of pyrethrum flowers, and when the British and Dutch East Indies were captured by the Japanese, important sources of derris also disappeared.

Persistence was regarded as the outstanding advantage of DDT, but right from the beginning, long before Rachel Carson's warnings in 1962, researchers were aware of the dangers of a residual insecticide to beneficial insects. Other organochlorines are aldrin and HCH (lindane). DDT is now banned in most countries; aldrin is either banned or heavily restricted; only lindane is available to amateur gardeners in this country.

In the 1950s, the first organophosphorus insecticides appeared. They were initially discovered as a result of wartime research into poison gases. These insecticides are of variable persistence, but generally of *much* shorter persistence than organochlorines (three months rather than ten years), and also of very variable toxicity: parathion is one of the most dangerous; malathion, available to amateurs in Britain, is one of the safest. They have a broad spectrum of activity, like organochlorines, but some are systemic, unlike organochlorines.

Carbamates appeared in the 1960s — a by-product of the motor-tyre industry. Other carbamates are used as weedkillers and fungicides. Like organophosphates, they vary in persistence and toxicity. Aldicarb is very nasty, carbaryl is much safer.

Synthetic pyrethroid insecticides are quite a recent development — from the 1970s onwards. They are chemically similar to natural pyrethrum, and are still regarded as the great hope for the future. You need about 10,000 times *less* deltamethrin than DDT to kill a housefly, it is less toxic to humans, and has short persistence. But, as with all the other types, the more they are used, the more quickly pests develop resistance to them.

# Fungicides

Like insecticides, fungicides have developed from simple inorganic compounds, through crude synthetic products, to very subtle ones. However, there are no naturally fungicidal plant extracts to compare with nicotine or derris.

The Greeks and Romans used sulphur to control rusts and moulds. In the nineteenth century, lime-sulphur was used to control powdery mildew. Sulphur-based products are still very much in use. Bordeaux mixture (copper sulphate and lime) was discovered in 1885: this, and other copper-sulphate preparations, such as Cheshunt compound, are also still widely used despite the risk of phytotoxicity (damaging the plant).

Calomel (mercurous chloride) is very toxic to plants, and has limited uses as a result, but despite being very poisonous to humans it is still available for amateur use.

Organomercury compounds were developed, which were relatively harmless to plants, but were even *more* toxic to humans, so are no longer used.

In the 1930s and 1940s, the dithiocarbamates were developed (*thio* is Greek for sulphur). Zineb, maneb, mancozeb, thiram and others, some specific in action, others 'broad-spectrum', dominated the market until systemic fungicides, such as Benomyl, appeared in the late 1960s.

# Herbicides

Varro, writing in the first century BC, refers to the use of 'amurca' — the residue left from olives after extracting the oil — as a weedkiller. It was poured around the bases of trees and 'wherever noxious weeds grow in the fields'. The 'active ingredient' was probably salt, which was often used in the past as a weedkiller.

Bordeaux mixture, already in use as a fungicide in the nineteenth century, was discovered to kill charlock growing among the vineyards. 'Selective' weedkillers began when copper sulphate was used in cereal crops — bouncing off the upright cereal leaves and landing on the broad-leaved weeds. Various inorganic compounds were used in this way, including ammonium sulphate and sulphuric acid. Other inorganic compounds, such as sodium chlorate and sodium arsenite, were used as total weedkillers.

The first organic herbicide, DNOC, was discovered in 1932, but this, like sulphuric acid, is very poisonous and tricky to handle. There were some fatalities. In the 1940s, growth regulator herbicides were developed. The natural plant hormone IAA (indolyl acetic acid) was found to kill broad-leaved weeds such as charlock in cereal crops. Chemically related compounds 2, 4-D and MCPA were found to be even more effective. There was a war on, labour was in short supply, and herbicides were in demand. Since then more than a hundred herbicides have been developed, with remarkably varied applications: total, selective, translocated (like the 'systemic' insecticides and fungicides), contact, residual, pre-emergent and post-emergent. All these are described in Chapter 5.

Most people must be aware of how the use of pesticides has rocketed in recent years. Along with all the criticism of them, it should be mentioned that they have improved! The two are not unrelated: their use has increased *because* they have improved; the more they are used, the greater the demand for improvement and so on. Everyone has heard the horror stories — untrained workers in the Third World spraying crops without wearing protective clothing, with pesticides so toxic that they are banned elsewhere; disasters such as the one at Bhopal where the factory making carbaryl blew up and poisoned the whole area; and the story of DDT which built up in concentration through the 'food chain' from insects to birds to mammals — and so many more.

At the turn of the century, insecticides were not used much, but lead arsenate might have been used at the rate of 100 kilograms per hectare; a synthetic pyrethroid might today be used at 10 *grams* per hectare. If lead arsenate had remained in use, and were still being used today in those quantities, there would be little left alive anywhere. Lead arsenate is a straightforward biocide, and a little of it will kill a human; bioresmethrin is really not very poisonous to humans, who would have to eat half a pound of it to do any serious harm.

The 'organic' movement started at a time when chemicals were just beginning to catch on, and without any doubt the chemical pesticides used earlier — mercury, lead, arsenic compounds, and then organochlorines — were very dangerous because of their extreme toxicity, or persistence, or both. There can be little doubt that modern pesticides are *much* safer. The problem is that as they have become safer, their use has increased to the point where we are completely surrounded by them.

The most recent piece of legal history regarding pesticide use in this country was the Control of Pesticides Regulations in 1986, which sets out, for the first time, legal rather than voluntary obligations for those who sell, supply, store, advertise or *use* pesticides.

For the gardener, the word *use* is of particular importance. It means that someone with a stash of DDT left over from when it was legal can no longer *use* it. This is welcome news — but nor can gardeners legally use home-made sprays made from soap, rhubarb leaves, nettles or cigarette butts, because these are not approved products either.

# 3
# Organic v. conventional

As a member of my local organic gardening group, I was asked to help out for a couple of years on the 'organic' stand at the annual gardening exhibition. It was dominated, as many of these events are, by double-glazing firms and other commercial interests, but there were a lot of plants even so, and most of them looked excellent. The depressing fact was that the only plants that did not look green, bushy, floribund and healthy were those on the 'organic' stand. They had all been raised by amateurs, many of them on window-sills rather than in commercial, heated glass-houses. There were plenty of excuses. There were banners and placards, information sheets and true believers everywhere and even an 'organic' pop-song, but the plants themselves let the side down. The absurd thing was that although they were described as 'organically grown', nearly all were in the same 'Levington'-type soil-less compost that everyone uses — a perfectly good growing medium, but denounced by organic standards because of its 'chemical' content.

So what *is* 'organic' gardening? Needless to say, there is disagreement within the organic movement concerning some things, and there are several organic standards other than those set by the Soil Association, which

are the purest. However, there are certain basic tenets to which 'organic' farmers and gardeners adhere. The following arguments are often encountered:

1. 'We should try to copy nature in our gardens. Plants should be considered not in isolation but as part of the garden as a whole — this includes the microscopic fungi and bacteria, worms, insects and other creatures in the soil, the birds and mammals and even the weeds. In nature, these are balanced, and plants are healthy.'

2. 'Chemicals should not be used because they upset this balanced ecology. Insecticides and fungicides harm beneficial creatures more than their targets, which leads to *more* pests and diseases in the long run.'

3. 'Artificial fertilizers cause rapid lush growth and this encourages pests and diseases.'

4. 'Weedkillers leave poisonous residues and weaken garden plants. Weeds should be put on the compost heap and recycled along with other plant debris.'

5. 'Compost feeds soil organisms which

make nutrients available to plants.'

Taking these points one by one, here are some obvious objections (also often encountered).

1. If you can find a genuinely 'natural' eco-system, and presumably this means one with no people in it, the complex web of competing plants and animals is stable and every species has its niche — for the sake of this argument, let us accept that premise. In this situation any weak or unhealthy specimen would not last five minutes. Unless we grow only wild flowers indigenous to our climate and soil, most of our garden plants are highly *un*natural hybrids or plants introduced from other countries, and they could not be expected to fend for themselves in our natural ecosystem.

2. 'Chemicals should not be used because. . .' This is the crux of the matter. All things are chemical, but some are more chemical than others, to misquote George Orwell. Most 'chemicals' are banned from the organic garden, but a few are allowed. How do these compare with the rest?

A garden is an artificial environment anyway, unless it has been uncultivated for years. The ecology of a garden is continually being disrupted by digging, crop rotation, adding compost selectively to one area at the expense of another, removing unwanted or diseased specimens, putting in new ones, tidying up, and removing dead material. The very act of cultivation is the first, and fundamental, act of disruption, and arguably it is what sets us apart from nature. But it is true that pesticides harm predators as well as pests, and in some cases this may actually increase the numbers of pests. Different pesticides have different effects and side-effects, which we will look into.

3. Artificial fertilizers may cause rapid,

lush growth if used in large amounts, particularly nitrogen fertilizers — but some organic fertilizers may also do so. If plants take up too much nitrogen, their tissues grow with thin walls which are more easily invaded by fungi or insects. A balanced supply of nutrients is generally best, but this is not the same as saying that *slow* growth is best. Many vegetable crops need to grow quickly — radishes and spinach for example — otherwise they will be hot and woody, tough and bitter. Sometimes a fertilizer boost will get a plant *through* a check in growth caused either by bad weather or by pest and disease attack. There is no reason why a plant growing very slowly should be more resistant to pests and diseases.

4. Weedkillers are as variable as other pesticides: some break down rapidly in the soil, others do not. Using the *wrong* weedkiller will *definitely* weaken garden plants, or even kill them, especially if used carelessly. However, competition from weeds weakens plants much more than weedkillers, and controlling weeds by pulling, digging or hoeing can also damage garden plants — onions in particular: careless hoeing dislodges them and pulling weeds by hand often brings the onion too!

5. Compost is without doubt wonderful stuff. But there is never *enough* of it, particularly if you are growing food crops. Almost every gardener has to get supplementary materials of some kind from an outside source.

If all these notions were simply true as stated then gardening the 'conventional' way would be impossible, which it evidently is not. But the implication is also that 'conventional' gardeners do not use anything *but* artifical fertilizers and pesticides. It is like suggesting that non-vegetarians eat nothing except meat. No sensible gardener would deliberately avoid recycling organic matter, or would always use weedkillers instead of a hoe or a hand. The question is: how important and how easy or difficult it is to get away without using *any* artificial aids, and when we make exceptions, what should they be?

There is no doubt that relying on, or over-use of, pesticides and artificial fertilizers can damage the environment. More and more people — gardeners, scientists, politicians and even farmers — accept it. It is useful to make a comparison with drugs. Drug companies exert pressures on doctors similar to those that agrochemical firms exert on farmers: the whole system is set up for their use. Some antibiotics — especially broad-spectrum — have become so overprescribed as to become almost useless because of pathogen resistance, and in the Third World there is a similar lack of control or understanding of their uses and effects, as with pesticides. Many people turn to 'alternative' medicine or 'holistic' approaches. But very few people in life-or-death situations deny the power of modern medicine. Very few people (there *are* some) would prevent their child taking a course of drugs that would save its life. We should not draw the analogy too closely — plants are not our children, and you can take cuttings to reproduce a plant, which is not possible (yet) with human beings. But it is a useful analogy. To say that pesticides and fertilizers are over-used, sometimes disastrously, is not the same thing as saying that using them is *always* wrong, any more than over-dependence on drugs negates the whole of western medicine.

The most common motto that defines organic gardening is 'Feed the soil, not the plant'. This means: put bulky manure or compost into the soil; this will be broken down by soil micro-organisms to provide plant nutrients, rather than giving the plant its nutrients directly by using artificial (soluble) fertilizers. As a general principle it is excellent; ignoring it, as most modern farmers do, leads to a gradual decrease in organic content in the soil and deterioration of the soil structure. But 'organic' gardeners break their own rules all the time by using liquid feeds, albeit of organic origin. What is the difference between an organic liquid feed and any other? They all give the plant what it needs in a hurry. Seaweed products claim to be 'biostimulant', which means they contain some growth hormones (cytokinins). In another context, a product containing 'hormones', even 'natural' ones, would be shunned by organic consumers. Think of the raging controversy about growth hormones in beef production.

Many people with small town gardens do not have any 'soil' to feed; gardening is all done in tubs, pots and planters. These are usually filled with peat/sand-based compost (if you do use soil in these situations, plants do not do very well!). It cannot matter too much whether the fertilizer added to the peat and sand is organic or not. There is no soil involved, so it cannot be damaged or improved. Most people use seed/potting compost either to grow plants in pots, or to propagate seeds or cuttings. One may make a political statement by not buying a multi-purpose compost manufactured by Fisons, and getting it from an 'organic' outlet instead, but it should not affect your plants or the environment very much either way. However, peat is a non-renewable resource which is rapidly being depleted, whereas the cow manure, which is added to the peat in organic types of compost, is not. The cow manure also provides humus which not only supplies nutrients in a slow release form but is also a good 'store' for any nutrients added later. So a good organic compost may well have some advantages over a purely peat-based one.

There are various organic standards; for growers and farmers, the 'unified organic standard' is applied by the Soil Association, whose inspectors visit their farms before their 'organic symbol of quality' can be awarded, shown in Fig. 4.

Fig 4: the Soil Association symbol

Under Soil Association rules, composts, slurries, pure seaweed products, fish meal, bonemeal, hoof and horn, wood ash, basic slag, rock phosphate, rock potash, feldspar, dolomite and limestone are permitted as fertilizers. Occasional use of a few others such as blood and potassium sulphate is allowed but everything else is banned. The only insecticides allowed are soap, pyrethrum, derris and quassia. No herbicides are allowed, but potassium permanganate, sulphur and cuprous (copper) oxide fungicides are permitted. Metaldehyde slug killer may be used as an impregnated tape, but not as bait pellets.

These are the rules, and if you want to grow and sell organic produce you have to obey them. But ordinary gardeners are not in business and can do as they please. I assume that anyone reading a book with 'green' in the title will be concerned with his or her own health and that of the environment, and will want to avoid using anything harmful. But the substances permitted by the Soil Association are poisons and fertilizers, just as are the substances banned by them.

What *is* the basis of this discrimination? Lawrence Hills, the godfather of British organic gardening, said in *Grow Your Own Fruit and Vegetables* that there is no point in using pesticides just because they are old-fashioned, but it seems in some ways that this is the basis for discrimination. Cuprous oxide is the copper fungicide permitted by the Soil Association, but most 'organic' gardeners use Bordeaux mixture, based on copper sulphate. It is a good example of a general biocide, albeit a weakish one; poisonous not just to fungi but to plants and animals, and *entirely* persistent. Before the development of other fungicides it was used so extensively that some orchards in Kent became so saturated with it that nothing would grow under the trees, there were no earthworms, the soil was completely poisoned. Compare this with Mancozeb, to take an example at random from the rest that are banned. It is many times less acutely toxic to mammals, more effective against most of the fungi that Bordeaux mixture is used for, does less damage to plants, is less dangerous to fish and does not persist for long in the environment. It is, however, a 'suspected carcinogen' — more on this later.

Weedkillers are banned completely, but ugly non-biodegradable plastic mulches are used. What is the net effect on the environment of a sheet of black polythene compared with an equivalent dose of herbicide? It is probably impossible to answer a question like that, but it is interesting to ponder. In Italy, the proliferation of plastic bags is a major pollution issue.

Pyrethrum, a plant extract permitted by the Soil Association, is an insecticide with the usual problems — it is harmful to most insects including bees, as well as the target insects. It has a further disadvantage: it is *so* non-persistent that it breaks down in sunlight or air, and becomes ineffective within a few hours. 'Organic' gardeners often use it mixed with derris, which is more persistent, to get round this problem. Bioresmethrin, a synthetic pyrethroid (pyrethrum-like), is less toxic to mammals and does not break down quite so quickly. It is synthetic and therefore banned by the Soil Association.

But nicotine, a *known* carcinogen, teratogen and mutagen and very deadly poison, was approved as an 'organic' product until quite recently — presumably on the grounds that it is 'natural'. There are already problems of pest resistance to some synthetic pyrethroid insecticides. This is a feature common to most poisons, which get used repeatedly and exclusively, and indeed *natural* pyrethrum is no exception.

A reason for avoiding pesticide sprays is that they may affect the taste of certain crops. Quassia, a tropical bark preparation used by 'organic' gardeners as an insecticide, acts partly as a deterrent, being very bitter to taste — not only for insects but for humans, too. If in doubt, do not eat a lettuce that has been sprayed with quassia in less than a couple of weeks!

It might seem at this point that I am advocating the use of chemicals. Not so. Hardly anything goes on my garden except farmyard manure and compost, and nothing else at all on my allotment where I grow food crops. My point is that poisons are poisons, whether manufactured by multi-national agrochemical companies, or by brewing up cigarette ends, and the effectiveness or nastiness is independent of that.

A major reason for not buying garden products, whether fertilizer or pesticide, is expense, and this applies equally to 'organic' or 'non-organic' products. I buy a trailer load of farmyard manure every two years to supply my 10 rod (approx 46 metres × 4.6 metres) allotment. This costs £24, i.e. £12 per year. Apart from seeds, my outgoings are minimal. If I bought fertilizers, weedkillers, fungicides and insecticides, and used them in the kind of quantities a farmer might use, I would probably spend a further £50 per year. I weed by hand, hoe and fork; I pick off caterpillars and squash aphids when I see them; everything else has to fend for itself. Anything that looks badly diseased or not growing well is pulled up. I am fortunate,

to some extent, that my steep piece of chalk hillside is blasted by salty gales, which blow a lot of pests away, and my allotment is remarkably pest-free. There are a lot of un-cultivated, weedy allotments nearby, which probably harbour many pest predators, but I still get bad carrot fly sometimes, plenty of slugs and snails, and a variety of potato diseases. Cabbages and cauliflowers consistently fail to reach a useful size; no doubt they would do better with some extra fertilizer. It is about as 'organic' as you can get, but this is partly due to lack of time: there is always so much to be done that is essential that I do not have time for spraying!

Things are slightly different in the garden. Occasionally the 'rules' get broken. We have used a selective aphicide when the aphids have got out of hand on the roses. We sometimes use a total weedkiller on the paving, and, yes, we have used slug pellets around the hostas. We do not eat the roses, so there is no danger of any aphicide getting into us, and pirimicarb is fairly harmless to other insects. Path weedkillers are not going to harm the soil or any garden plants, because it is only the cracks between paving slabs that are involved. However, slug pellets are more of an issue: if animals eat the pellets, they may suffer, and if birds or frogs or hedgehogs eat the dead slugs, they may, too. Slug pellets contain a pet-repellent these days, and there is some evidence that birds are canny enough not to eat dead slugs that taste of metaldehyde. However, nothing else has worked, so it is either that or no hostas. Slugs and snails are the organic gardener's biggest headache.

There are numerous techniques for poisonless pest control — this book will not go into detail as there are so many other books devoted to the subject, but some of the methods are outlined in the last chapter. This book is intended to present the issues, so that whatever fertilizers or poisons you decide to use, or not to use, you have a clear idea of what you are doing and why.

'Organic' gardeners tend to represent all others as using masses of chemicals. No one with any sense would do that, but even now the manufacturers of chemicals seem to try to make out they are all you need. The question is: where do you draw the line? Draw the line where you will, but it is useful to know why you are drawing it there, and to distinguish between the rational and emotional reasons for doing something: if you feel better after a day of digging or hoeing than after a day of spraying, that

cannot be bad! I do.

But when you buy your little plastic bottle of high potash liquid feed for your tomatoes, think of the environmental impact involved in the manufacture of the plastic bottle, packing several bottles into cardboard cartons, forwarding them by truck to the wholesaler, then the retailer, incinerating the bottle after its disposal. In the light of this, is it really crucial whether the little $K^+$ potassium ions that your ripening tomatoes crave come from processed seaweed ('organic') or processed rock ('non-organic')?

# 4
# Soils, fertilizers and plant growth

*N*atural soils, before being cultivated by humans, evolved over hundreds, thousands or tens of thousands of years by the interaction of climate, vegetation and animals on the landscape, and the rocks that composed it. You cannot separate the processes. Once started, each factor has an effect on the other: as the soil evolves it influences what grows on it, and this can influence the climate, which in turn affects the other processes. The most famous example of what happens when the natural process is disrupted is the tropical rainforest. When the mighty trees are felled, all that remains is a mass of tree stumps and a little vegetation which is exposed to the full blast of the sun and rain. All the processes of recycling nutrients by animals and plants, large or microscopic, are halted, the rain washes the soil away, and the sun scorches what remains. This in turn affects the climate. The moisture held by all those trees is gone, so it can no longer be drawn up into clouds to fall as rain elsewhere. In a few years the area is scrub or even semi-desert, and the climate of surrounding areas is altered too.

In Britain, we are fortunate not to have the problem of an extreme climate. If we did, no doubt Europe would have been a desert long ago. Our environment has been used,

abused, cultivated for so long, and survives, continually changing. The chalk downs were once covered with native hardwood trees: beech, ash, elm which were felled long ago. Sheep farming dominated the area until recently, and the downland turf that ecologists and environmentalists seek to preserve is the product of that form of agriculture. Since the Second World War more and more downland has been given over to cereal monoculture. Still it survives, apparently. Many downland hill tops appear to have no soil at all. In spring, barley sprouts from a white chalk desert, supported by rain and chemical fertilizer alone. It is possible to support some crops with big yields on a large scale with hardly any soil. But you could not do it in Amazonia, and you could not grow cauliflowers or runner beans like that, even in England.

Even if soil has not been eroded to nothing, thousands of years of cultivation have changed it. There are no 'natural' soils in Britain. However, soils generally retain some of the qualities they started with, even in your back garden. There is the parent rock: chalk, sandstone, clay, or granite; this may be deep down or very close to the surface. On this is the subsoil, which may be a metre deep or almost non-existent, but derives from the parent rock, with some organic matter in it, and on top of that is the topsoil. This may be only 10 cm deep and virtually sit on the parent rock. Chalk downland is often like this, or may be half a metre deep and blend very gradually into the subsoil. The topsoil is the section in which most of the living processes go on. Deep, water-collecting roots may penetrate down to, or into, the parent rock, but the feeding roots are mostly confined to the top 15 cm. The minerals in your soil originally come from the parent rock. The minerals are, in fact, everything that plants require to grow, apart from carbon, oxygen, hydrogen and nitrogen which derive from water or air. If these are lacking, they have to be added in some form. Where soils are cultivated for crops, the amount of minerals taken out every year far exceeds the amount made available by natural soil-forming processes.

The mineral part of a soil is a mixture of *sand, silt* and *clay*. Whichever of these dominates, determines the character of the soil. The distinction between the three is somewhat arbitrary, but sand is defined as being particles between 0.02 mm (two-hundredths of a millimetre) and 2 mm. Silt particles are smaller than sand, and larger than clay. Clay particles are smaller than 0.002 mm (two thousandths of a millimetre). For reasons that come under the heading of 'physics', water cannot percolate through the tiny gaps between particles of this size, so the clay holds water — but not in the way that a sponge or peat holds water, because you cannot squeeze it out. This makes clay a very special substance, and a vital ingredient in soil. But more than about 30 per cent of clay means that the soil gets waterlogged, is unable to breath. It is not only very hard to cultivate but is a very difficult medium in which to grow plants.

Sometimes clay is the parent rock of a soil, so even if the topsoil has been well cultivated, it remains waterlogged, because water

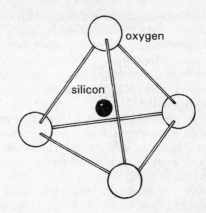

Fig 5: a silicon tetrahedron

cannot drain through the underlying clay. Digging a soakaway or laying land drains can help with this problem.

A soil that is mostly sand has the opposite problem — water and nutrients drain straight through it.

A 'loam' is the ideal soil, with well-balanced proportions of clay, silt and sand. It is well drained and aerated, but also reasonably moisture- and nutrient-retentive.

Apart from its ability to hold moisture, clay is special in other ways and, at the risk of being over-technical, some space is now devoted to it. Most rocks (with the notable

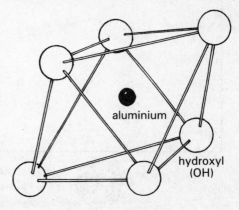

Fig 6: an aluminium octahedron

exception of limestone or chalk, which are composed of the remains of marine animals that dropped to a prehistoric sea-bed) are composed of *silicates*. The basic building block is the silicon tetrahedron — a pyramid of oxygen atoms with a silicon atom in the middle (see Fig. 5).

These pyramids are packed together as crystals, with various other cations, such as iron, aluminium, calcium and magnesium, packing them out to form different crystalline structures. Grains of sand or silt are small pieces of this hard, inert crystal. Sometimes they form a sheet structure called a silica sheet. Similar sheets are formed from the aluminium octahedron, a kind of double pyramid (see Fig. 6).

The rocks from which clays come are composed of various combinations of alumina and silica sheets. When these break down, the tiny particles that remain, instead of being more or less round like grains of sand, are thin, flat sheets stacked together rather like lasagne. The important thing about these tiny sheets is that, like sheets of

lasagne, they have a lot of *surface area*. Imagine a sheet of A4 paper, which is about 20 cm by 30 cm. If you take both sides of it, this total surface area is about 1,200 square centimetres. Now crumple it up into a ball. It is the same piece of paper, so it is the same *size*, but its surface area is much smaller (see Fig. 7).

The process of 'chemical weathering', which reduces these rocks to particles less than two millionths of a metre across, leaves a lot of 'free energy' around. This makes the flat surfaces sticky and they 'adsorb' particles around them. In addition to this, they have a negative electrical charge, which makes them attractive to any cations nearby.

This is not a science book, nor is it a cook book, but let us compare clay particles with lasagne again. Flat sticky sheets of pasta are covered with nutritious sauce; since the lasagne has several layers, there is sauce in between the layers as well as on top and bottom. Just as you can make a lasagne with green or white pasta, or in alternating layers, and alternating meat or cheese sauces in

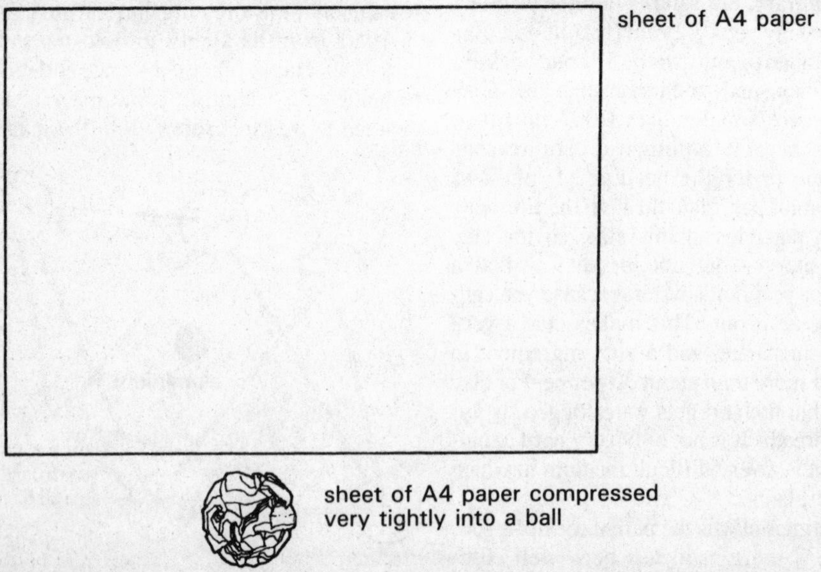

sheet of A4 paper

sheet of A4 paper compressed
very tightly into a ball

Fig 7: surface area

34

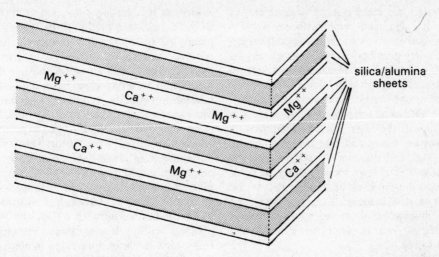

Fig 8: typical structure of a clay particle

between, so can clays vary in structure (see Fig. 8).

If you include the surfaces between the layers as well as the outside, some types of clay have surfaces up to 800 square metres per gram! And if you remember that each bit of surface is covered with calcium, magnesium, potassium ions and other particles adsorbed to it, you see why the clay portion of a soil affects its fertility so much.

In addition, any cations removed from the surfaces can be replaced by others, in a kind of exchange system. So if fertilizer is added to the soil, the clay particles can hold it. Clays vary in their ability to do this, and soil scientists give it a name — *cation exchange capacity* or CEC.

If a soil contains no clay, it is unable to cling onto or adsorb nutrients. If a soil contains just a little clay, it may be 'saturated' and still hold few nutrients.

Farmers have been adding clay to soil (marling) at least since Roman times: Pliny (AD 61-113) described it. Although a heavy clay soil is one of the hardest to deal with (adding lime helps break it up, a process called 'flocculation'), a soil with no clay is

no soil at all. You can grow plants without soil, without going into hydroponics, just by growing houseplants in ordinary peat-based compost. You feed them with a mixture of soluble chemical fertilizer, and they grow very well. You can grow tomatoes in grow-bags, and get very good crops. But you have to keep feeding them because there is no clay to act as a reservoir, and you have to give them feed diluted by just the right amount because there is no reservoir to take up the excess, or 'buffer' the input.

An even more essential ingredient is organic content. In a natural soil this forms as the 'litter' of dead vegetable or animal waste decomposes on the surface, and then is drawn into the soil, by earthworms, beetles, etc., assisted by fungi and bacteria. Each process of decomposition makes it finer until it reaches the stage called 'humus'. Humus is comparable to clay in many ways, but it has most of the advantages of clay without the disadvantages. In a heavy clay soil it will bind onto clay particles and effectively break it up, making it more freely drained — the effect is similar to adding lime. In a sandy soil it will bind to the sand particles and make it more water retentive. Humus also has a large surface-to-volume ratio and cation exchange capacity, like clay, and being decomposed vegetable matter, the ions it contains are those that plants require. The only problem with humus is that it gets used up and must be constantly replenished.

In cultivated soils this natural process is disrupted: the litter is usually removed — lawns are mown and raked, vegetables are cropped and dug up — and may not be replaced. The lawn mowings may be composted but put back on another part of the garden; dead branches of trees are burnt; and the ultimate fate of any vegetables consumed by the gardener is usually down the loo and out to sea.

One way or another the losses must be replaced. It can take thousands of years for a soil to form, for those rocks to be converted by frost, sun, oxidation, fungal and bacterial attack into minerals in the soil available to plants. They can be removed very much more quickly.

One of the cornerstones of 'organic' philosophy is that they must be replaced by means as close to 'natural' as possible. This means compost or animal manure and the use of legumes to fix nitrogen, and, if this is not enough, by rock phosphate and rock potash. These are simply the rocks which the fertilizer industry uses to extract the manufactured products which are soluble and immediately available to the plant. The other major nutrient, nitrogen, cannot be mined because it exists as a gas in the atmosphere.

Let us compare the processes that happen in the soil when nutrients are added as chemical fertilizers, and in an 'organic' way.

*Nitrogen* The nitrogen in compost or manure is first broken down by microbes and enzymes to ammonium ($NH_4^+$), which can be retained by the soil colloids (glue-like substances, i.e. clay and humus), and can be used by plants to a certain extent in that form.

Most of it is further converted to nitrate ($NO_3^-$), and this is the form in which plants take up most of their nitrogen. Other sources are various nitrogen-fixing organisms. The most well-known of these is the Rhizobium bacteria, which has a symbiotic relationship with the root-hairs of legumes. The bacteria feeds on carbohydrates from the plant roots and supplies nitrogen in return, which it has 'fixed' from the air. This is the most important natural source of nitrogen other than animal manure — although a significant amount is deposited as nitric acid created by lightning flashes! Not all strains of Rhizobium are nitrogen fixing, and low pH (high acidity), lack of calcium and especially high levels of nitrate can inhibit the formation of the 'nodules' that develop on the root hairs. There are also 'free living', nitrogen-fixing organisms whose activity is also suppressed by high levels of nitrogen already present.

Because of this, when artificial nitrogen fertilizers are added bacterial nitrogen fixing is suppressed. This is used as an argument against using chemical fertilizers, though if a nitrogen-rich manure were applied before planting beans or peas, it would have a similar effect. Where soil is acid. or is known to be deficient in Rhizobium, legume seed can be coated with the bacteria before sowing. Applying nitrogen as a nitrate fertilizer causes a well-known problem — leaching. Because nitrate ($NO_3^-$) is an anion, it is less well held by the clay-humus colloid, and is quickly washed out. This is not only wasteful, but may cause problems to the water supply. Applying nitrogen as ammonium ($NH_4^+$) causes *acidification* as it breaks down to nitrate. For those who like chemical equations, it is very simply expressed:

$$NH_4^+ + 2O_2 \rightarrow NO_3^- + H_2O + 2H^+$$

Notice the two 'H pluses' at the end of the

equation. They mean acid! The final disadvantage of chemical fertilizers is that the concentrated salt solution created as the granules dissolve can scorch young roots, so care has to be taken when and where the granules are placed, but you can get similar problems with organic manures also if their nitrogen level is very high.

*Phosphorus* is the next main nutrient. Ground rock phosphate and bonemeal are the 'organic' gardener's supply over and above compost and manure. The rock might be fluorapatite ($Ca_{10}(PO_4)_6F_2$) which is insoluble. Finely ground it is slowly broken down with the aid of micro-organisms to supply the phosphate ions ($H_2PO_4^-$), which the plant requires. Symbiotic associations of rock and fungi called mycorrhizas — comparable to the nitrogen-fixing Rhizobium — help plants to absorb phosphate when it is in short supply. This activity, like that of Rhizobium, is suppressed by the addition of phosphate fertilizer to a soil. Mycorrhizas also enhance plants' uptake of zinc and copper, and this is a suggested reason for their deficiency in some phosphate fertilized crops. But composted manure also contains plenty of phosphate and this has the same effect.

There are also soil bacteria which break down the organic phosphate compounds that come from dead plant and animal debris, and convert them into mineral phosphate, but most of this is absorbed by the micro-organisms themselves. It must be remembered that these wonderful soil organisms are consumers as well as suppliers; the whole soil environment is immensely competitive; soil bacteria and fungi are not there simply to make life easier for the plant; many of them are in direct competition with plants and some are parasitic and therefore harmful.

Triplesuperphosphate is a typical phosphate fertilizer produced by dissolving rock phosphate in acid: it is $Ca(H_2PO_4)_2$, and is soluble in water. However, when granules of this dissolve in the soil they produce a very acid solution — pH even as low as 1.5 — which reacts with other soil minerals and dissolves large amounts of aluminium, manganese and iron. After about a day, the *soluble* phosphate fertilizer has become a variety of *insoluble* calcium, iron and aluminium phosphates. Exactly what these are depends on the mineral content of the soil and its acidity, but over-application of soluble phosphates can cause valuable minor nutrients to become 'locked up'. They are, however, released again by microbes, along with the phosphates, so it is not really a shock-horror story. It is estimated that only 10 to 20 per cent of fertilizer phosphate is absorbed by plants in the first year, the rest remaining as fertilizer reaction products.

*Potassium* is the other major nutrient. The 'rock potash' — adularian shale — approved by organic gardeners is so insoluble and slow-acting that a Henry Doubleday Research Association (HDRA) report admitted that it seems to make no difference at all! If you use a complete 'organic' fertilizer containing hoof and horn for nitrogen, bonemeal for phosphate, and rock potash, the soil might well suffer from a potassium deficiency because the potash is so 'slow-release' that it is effectively non-active. Many 'organic' fertilizers contain seaweed, which is a good source of potassium and is readily available to plants.

This brings us to the 'chemical' potassium fertilizers. Potassium chloride ('muriate of potash') comprises the main part of the salt deposits from which they come and is cheaper; potassium sulphate (sulphate of potash) is better for crops such as potatoes and beetroot which do not like the chloride part. Potassium fertilizers do not arouse such controversy as the others because they do not normally leach out like nitrogen or cause acidification, and they do not lock up other elements in the way phosphates do.

A problem that can occur, however, in any situation is that an excess of one mineral can lead to a deficiency or non-availability of another. Magnesium, calcium and potassium are chemically similar and essential cations. They have a sort of pecking order on the exchange surfaces of the clay/humus colloid. The first cation to be leached out of a soil is sodium, followed by potassium, magnesium and calcium. When these are gone aluminium and, finally, hydrogen remain, at which point you have a completely useless acid soil! On chalk or limestone soils, calcium not only dominates in this way, but also by sheer quantity: there is so much free calcium that other essential minerals often do not get a look in. Magnesium and iron deficiencies are a common problem, leading to chlorosis, which is a yellowing between the leaf veins — on new leaves with iron deficiency, on older leaves with magnesium deficiency. This is because iron and magnesium are essential for the production of chlorophyll, which gives leaves their green colour.

It is clear that soil is an immensely complex and variable substance, in which everything depends on everything else, in which the living and the mineral are involved in intricate and constant interaction. It is possible to treat it as though it were merely a sponge to hold added chemicals and as an anchor for plant roots — witness the barley growing out of the chalk — and if your garden consists of pots and tubs alone, it is perfectly reasonable. But it is wasteful and ultimately destructive of the soil. Once a soil has lost the structure, which is dependent on its organic content, it ceases to hold nutrients or provide a suitable medium for plant roots. It must be better to treat soil as alive, and to imitate the natural cycle of growth and decay as closely as possible. However, if this approach is taken to its extreme, nothing should be added except compost.

The beauty of compost, rightly the rave of all good gardeners, is that, being mostly decomposed plant material, it has all the nutrients necessary for plant growth in an available but long-lasting form, and is of an ideal, near neutral pH. The problem is that, like anything marvellous, there is never enough of it. There are always greedy plants — especially vegetable crops — that demand more than limited supplies of compost can supply, especially in spring. When the weather warms up and everything starts to grow there is intense competition, including those very important micro-organisms. They can steal the nutrients from the plants!

It is common to boost the nitrogen supply, especially to leaf crops, to get them established. This is against the principles of 'organic' gardeners, and even the use of dried blood, though permitted, is frowned upon because it is too quick-acting, that is, too soluble and so too much like a 'chemical' fertilizer, depriving soil micro-organisms of their role in making nutrients available to plants. Can this, or the use of a chemical fertilizer for that matter, really be inexcusable? The motto is 'feed the soil, not the plant' and yet most 'organic' gardeners accept the practice of giving liquid manure or seaweed feeds to those favoured plants that need extra attention. Liquid seaweed feeds are claimed to be 'biostimulant' — and indeed it is very likely that seaweed *is* a very good plant food, but surely following the 'Feed the soil, not the plant' rule it should be inexcusable to use anything so efficient! Urine is one of the best plant foods — expecially diluted 3:1 — and it is both natural *and* completely soluble. It is the ultimate chemical fertilizer, containing urea and potassium and phosphate ions in completely soluble form, along with a good supply of trace elements. Should cows on organic farms be restrained?

The fear that chemicals will kill or inhibit all soil micro-organisms should be allayed by the fact that many of the substances disapproved of for direct use on the soil are all right for putting on the compost heap, which is, of course, a mass of microbial action. Ammonium sulphate acts just as well as blood as a compost-heap activator. Different chemicals suppress different micro-organisms. With the reduction of competition from one area, others thrive. Some fungicides are known to suppress the population of nitrifying bacteria or Rhizobium, others actually *encourage* useful bacteria by suppressing competition from others.

Research done in America comparing an organic farm (no chemicals used since 1907) with a conventional farm revealed a far *higher* level of nitrifying bacteria on the conventional farm; seven times as many nitrosomonas, three times as many nitrobacter (these are the bacteria that convert $NH_4$ to $NO_3$).

No doubt agrochemical firms and other vested interests — particularly in America where most university research is sponsored by large companies — exert considerable influence, and have scientific reports produced to prove that their way is best and that 'organic' farming (or gardening) is actually harmful. But the limited amount of research done so far about the influence of soil micro-organisms on plant productivity is inconclusive. To complicate the matter, it is known that plant roots exude their own chemicals which interfere with micro-organisms as well!

How to conclude? There is little doubt that relying on chemical fertilizer *instead* of recycling organic waste is destructive in the long term, but whether using small amounts of chemicals in addition to compost and manure is harmful seems a matter for speculation. The organic approach will definitely do no harm, but if you are growing vegetables you will need a great deal of compost — which you can get only by depriving another area of the garden or by importing something from outside.

Having devoted considerable space to the elements on which plants grow, we should now have a look at the plants themselves. Plants grow in two media — the soil and the atmosphere. The soil must have air for the chemical and biochemical processes within it, and roots also need air to function properly — so the atmosphere actually goes down some way below that apparently hard surface of the soil. Both halves of a plant — the roots, and the stem and leaves — supply each other, and each mirrors the functions of the other. The stem supports the leaves and flowers in the air; the main roots support the network of minor roots and root hairs in the soil. Water and minerals are drawn up to the leaves from the roots; the leaves supply the products of photosynthesis, such as sugars, down to the rest of the plant. The processes are vastly complicated and can never be explained, any more than you can explain why water feels wet, but it is worth describing a little of what goes on because fertilizers and pesticides get onto or into plants in various ways.

*Transpiration, diffusion* and *osmosis* are words of which most people have heard. They are all 'passive' processes which partly account for the movement of water and dissolved substances around plants. When water evaporates from leaves, as it does on any normal day, and especially on warm and windy days, it leaves a deficit which has to be replaced. Water — actually sap, a solution of minerals — is thus drawn up through the plant from the roots, creating a *transpiration* stream. Under normal conditions, water cannot be raised up in a column more than 30 metres high, but somehow plants are able to do it — Sequoia sempervirens, the redwood tree, may grow to 100 metres!

How the sap solution gets into the plant is explained by *osmosis*. First: diffusion. If you put a teaspoon of salt in a cup of water it dissolves and eventually the water becomes equally salty throughout, even without stirring. This is diffusion. The $Na^+$ and $Cl^-$

ions move from a strong solution at the bottom of the teacup to a weaker solution at the top until they reach equilibrium. Osmosis is a special type of diffusion. It involves a semi-permeable membrane — that is, one that lets some things through but not others, water, for example, but not salt. If you put a little bag made of a semi-permeable membrane, partly filled with salty water, into a cup of water, the salt cannot get out into the water through the membrane, but the water can get in, so the bag of salt solutions fills up with water, making a larger amount of weaker solution.

Plant cell walls are semi-permeable membranes, and this mechanism roughly explains movement of water through plant tissues. Whenever there is a relative shortage of water, water is drawn in and moves, with a chain effect, from cell to cell. Once it reaches the xylem tissue (see page 43) it is simply drawn up in the transpiration stream. This is only part of the story. Perhaps because plants have no arms and legs or brains, there has been resistance to the idea that plants have any *active* processes. But plant physiologists now agree that various active processes must go on because things happen in plants that cannot be otherwise accounted for. It is thought that some ions get into plants passively, along with the water, and others have to be actively transported by little chemically driven pumps.

Where crops are grown using the Nutrient Film Technique — a method often used in glasshouses for growing tomatoes or strawberries — their roots just dangle in a perfectly balanced solution of everything they need. The proportions are constantly monitored and adjusted as required. But plants do not need these conditions to grow! If plants took in minerals only in the proportions in which they were available, then seaweed would be full of sodium chloride, common salt. There is 40 times as much sodium in the sea as potassium, but seaweed contains about six times as much potassium as sodium. This is why seaweed is such a useful high potassium plant food. But plants do not necessarily discriminate in favour of useful minerals: a certain type of chickweed, Holosteum umbellatum, when growing in soil rich in mercury salts, accumulates them in such concentration that it is said to have droplets of metallic mercury within its cells. Until recently it was feared that vegetables would take up the lead emitted by car exhausts, but it is now established that this is not a problem. Even where there is a high concentration of lead in the soil, for example in city gardens, plants still take up very little of it.

Not only are plants different from people in not having arms and legs and brains, but also in the most fundamental way. They are *autotrophs* rather than *heterotrophs*. This means that they derive their existence entirely from non-living sources. Animals eat plants or other animals; they cannot eat carbon, oxygen, nitrogen or metals in their simple form, but for plants this is the only way.

Photosynthesis has been investigated in depth and out of depth since 1796, when a scientist called Ingen-Housz suggested that plants obtain their carbon from carbon dioxide in the air. Enough has been written about it to fill a library, and a vast amount is known about the biochemical pathways involved. But the bottom line is that life is created out of not-life according to this chemical equation, which actually conceals an incredibly intricate series of intermediate steps:

$$CO_2 + H_2O \xrightarrow{\text{sunlight}} CH_2O + O_2$$

Carbon dioxide plus water makes, with the energy of sunlight, sugar and oxygen. This happens wherever plants are green, and mostly on the top side of leaves. It is not a simple reaction that you could copy in a chemistry laboratory by dissolving carbon dioxide gas in water — all you would get from that would be carbonated water as in fizzy drinks.

The sugar produced by photosynthesis is the basic substance from which other plant materials derive, but some of it is kept as an energy supply to drive the plant's various functions. When needed, it breaks down into carbon dioxide and water again, releasing the energy which was once sunlight.

$$CH_2O + O_2 \rightarrow H_2O + CO_2 + energy$$

This is called respiration, and is basically the photosynthesis process in reverse. Again, there is a complicated series of steps involved; if that were not the case, the sudden release of energy would kill the plant. It happens throughout the plant wherever energy is required, particularly where the plant is in active growth producing young roots and shoots. One of the most important agents in energy transfer in plants — and in all living things — is a molecule called adenosine tri-phosphate (ATP). By dropping one of its phosphates it becomes adenosine di-phosphate (ADP), and releases large amounts of energy. The *phosphate* in this process accounts for a plant's requirement for phosphate in its nutrient supply. Photosynthesis and respiration are very closely linked, and a common mode of action for herbicides and fungicides is to disrupt one or both of them.

To return to the leaf: the top surface, or cuticle, is waxy (sometimes hairy) and fairly resistant to water and anything else that falls on it. The bottom side is full of pores called stomata (one stoma, two stomata), which let in and out carbon dioxide, oxygen and water vapour from photosynthesis and respiration. Just as an animal has a soft underbelly, the lower side of a leaf is where it is most vulnerable. If water and air can get in and out, so can other things. This is why aphids, which are sap-suckers, tend to gather on the underside of the leaf; they simply put their proboscis (tongue) through the stomata, and feed. They, and many other pests, are protected by the leaf from weather and preda-

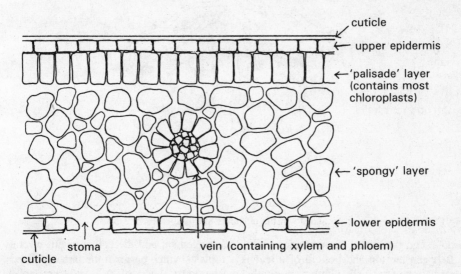

cuticle
upper epidermis
'palisade' layer (contains most chloroplasts)
'spongy' layer
lower epidermis
stoma
cuticle
vein (containing xylem and phloem)

Fig 9: typical section of a leaf

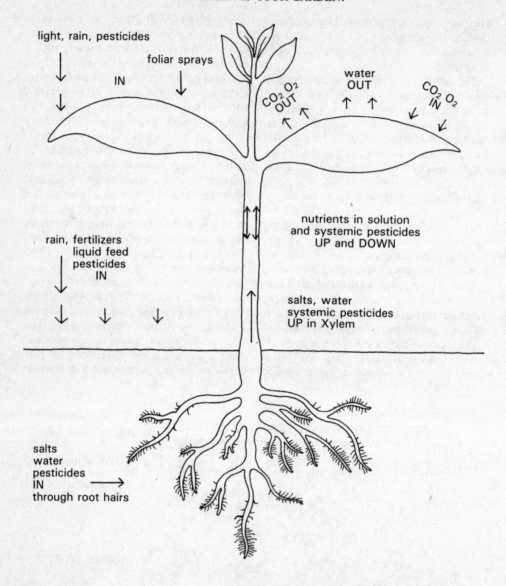

Fig 10: the ways in, out, up and down for nutrients and pesticides in a plant

tors — and the eye of the gardener.

Between the top and bottom of a leaf is a collection of basically similar cells called mesophyll. The top layer is a fairly orderly arrangement and the cells are full of chloroplasts which perform the photosynthesis. The lower layer of cells is less densely packed with plenty of spaces to allow the passage of water and gases — rather like a sponge. The standard drawing of the cross-section of a leaf is shown in Fig. 9.

This is the factory. It needs a transport system to supply and remove raw materials and products, and in the leaf the veins do this by connecting to the midrib which eventually leads back via the leaf stalk and branches to the main stem and roots. In plumbing terminology, the feed and return pipes go everywhere together. The 'feed' pipes are called xylem, the 'return' pipes are called phloem. The xylem brings up a solution of minerals (nitrate, phosphate, potassium, etc.) which are all required directly or indirectly in turning the glucose manufactured in the leaves into all the other components — cellulose, fats, proteins, etc. — that make up a plant. The phloem brings these products to where they are required — usually down. However, when a leaf ages and begins to die the useful materials in it are transported back up again to where they are of more use. How the plant knows where to send the various substances manufactured in the leaves is a complete mystery — just like its ability to choose which minerals it needs from the soil solution.

The purpose of this lightning trip through plant physiology, full of omissions and over-simplifications, is to give a general idea of how plants take in substances. Note that, unlike animals, they have no means of excreting waste products.

The simplest way to disrupt a plant is to put salt on it — as people discovered a long time ago. The salt immediately starts to dissolve in the leaf's moisture and by osmosis sucks the moisture from it, effectively 'scorching' it. Similarly in the soil, roots get scorched. Excessive nitrate can do the same thing whether in the form of raw manure or a chemical fertilizer. Lawn sand — a weed-killer/lawn food largely superseded now but still used by some people — works on this principle. Sand is mixed with ammonium

sulphate (and ferrous sulphate for moss control) which lands on the flat surfaces of broad-leaved weeds and damages them, but misses the more upright leaves of grass. By the time the ammonium sulphate has washed down to the grass roots it is sufficiently dilute to act as a fertilizer rather than a poison. A rather hit-and-miss affair!

Slight overdoses of nitrate simply get drawn into the plant from the soil solution; spinach and lettuce grown commercially often have very high levels of free nitrate, which causes concern because nitrates become nitrites in mammal stomachs and are, it is suspected, carcinogenic.

With the exception of foliar sprays (and plain water), the substances gardeners apply to leaves are poisons, either to kill the plant or to kill some other creature that is on the leaf: fungus, mollusc or insect. Despite the protective, waxy 'cuticle' on the top of leaves, they are surprisingly permeable, and can be fed as well as damaged. Plants can take in all the nutrients they require through their leaves, and foliar spraying has been an accepted way of feeding plants for many years now. This method bypasses all the normal processes for getting the required soluble salts from the soil through the roots and up the xylem tissues, as described earlier. But because the nutrients are taken in directly by the leaves, it is the leaves that benefit primarily. This is fine for plants in their vegetative phase of growth — that is, before they start to flower — and for plants such as cabbages and spinach whose leaves are the part for which the plant is grown. It is also a recommended way of instantly correcting any trace element deficiency in established plants (see Chelates in the A to Z).

It is always recommended to stop foliar spraying when a plant begins flowering — for instance when growing tomatoes — because encouraging leaf growth tends to inhibit flower and, therefore, fruit production. Ordinary liquid feeding to the roots can be continued. Foliar spraying, of course, breaks the organic gardeners' injunction to 'Feed the soil, not the plant' in the most absolute way, though organic gardeners do it all the time, content in the knowledge that they are using an 'organic' fertilizer.

# 5
# *Pesticides*

*I*n this situation, the only adequate response is to thank God for chemical pesticides and use them liberally. Unfortunately the strongest and most effective ones keep being withdrawn from the market on the grounds that they have been found to damage the environment. So when you hit on a really lethal sort, it's a good plan to buy it in large supply, which will allow you to go on using it after it has been outlawed. I did this for several seasons with a splendid product, now alas unobtainable, which wiped out everything from snails to flea beetles. It had no adverse effect on the bird population so far as I could see, though the neighbourhood cats did start to look a bit seedy.

John Cary wrote this in 1980 in *The Sunday Times*, continuing the article with a diatribe against cats.

No gardening writer would dare write anything like that any more, however wittily expressed. But by way of introduction to the chapter, it illustrates two points. First, the effectiveness of pesticides tends to be directly related to their dangerousness — though, as we shall see, this is not necessarily the case. Secondly, since the new regulations of 1986,

it is no longer permitted to use pesticides that have been withdrawn.

There are far more pesticides available to farmers and commercial growers than to amateur gardeners. Many of the active ingredients are the same (though those considered more dangerous are not available for amateur use), but products designed for gardeners are formulated so that they can be used 'easily, conveniently, safely and effectively', to quote the *Directory of Garden Chemicals*, published by the British Agrochemicals Association, which represents the interests of the bigger pesticide manufacturers in Britain. The word *formulated* is important. Not only does this involve the form that the pesticide comes in — powder, liquid, solution, suspension or granules — but also the proportion of active ingredients. Many amateur products are simply weaker versions of the professional ones.

These warning symbols appear, under EEC law, on all kinds of products which could be considered in some way dangerous (see Fig. 11).

Only the first three, if any, of these symbols will be found on garden chemicals: irritant, harmful and oxidizing. It is strange that the first two have the same symbol. How do you define toxic as opposed to harmful? The

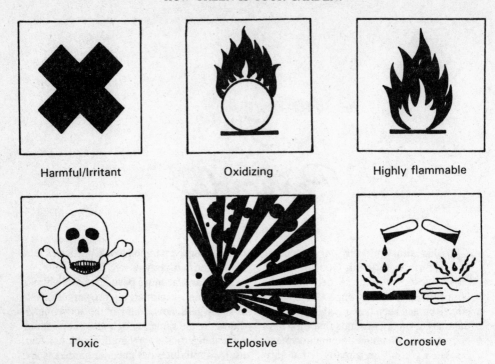

Harmful/Irritant · Oxidizing · Highly flammable

Toxic · Explosive · Corrosive

Fig 11: warning symbols

differences are necessarily arbitrary. Almost anything can be considered harmful under certain circumstances or in sufficient quantity. But it is interesting that paraquat, one of the deadliest chemicals, is still available to the amateur as an ingredient of ICI Pathclear and ICI Weedol. Surely such a product should be considered toxic and have the alarming skull-and-crossbones symbol on the packet? In fact it has no warning at all, not even the 'harmful' or 'irritant' cross symbol. The answer from ICI is simple: they contain very little of the active ingredient. Weedol contains only 2.5 per cent paraquat, with 2.5 per cent diquat. By the time this is further diluted with the required amount of water, you have a solution with *very* little paraquat in it.

Since the Control of Pesticides Regulations of 1986, we are not allowed to use anything

at all as pesticides except those approved by the Ministry of Agriculture, Fisheries and Food (MAFF), not even home-made soap sprays or elder concoctions. It is very unlikely that anyone is actually going to be prosecuted for using an unregistered soap insecticide, but it does mean that firms who have registered a soap product will do good business!

There is a standard way of measuring how poisonous something is. The substance is given to rats, most commonly orally but also inhaled, intravenously, on the skin, in the eye, or injected into various organs. The amount that kills 50 per cent of the sample is known as the Lethal Dose 50 per cent, or LD50 for short. This is measured in milligrams per kilogram. So if a rat weighs (say) 1 kilogram and the LD50 is 1,000 milligrams per kilogram, then a dose of 1,000 milligrams would kill half the rats tested. The *lower* the LD50 figure, the more poisonous the substance. Of course, you get different results each time you do the test, and LD50 figures vary quite a lot. Rats are used because, generally, they seem to react comparably, kilo for kilo, with humans. It is essential to remember that LD50s relate to the active ingredient, the pure stuff, neat. Pesticides are not usually formulated neat, they are mixed with various other substances and before use are usually further diluted, so that the spray contains a relatively small proportion of active ingredient — as we saw with the paraquat in ICI Weedol.

Not only that, but different ways of applying a poison have different problems. Granules — for instance for soil application at sowing time — are minimally hazardous to the person applying them: the same active ingredient used as a spray — especially in the very fine sprays used commercially — may present all manner of problems: it will get on to the user's skin, into eyes and lungs (if used without proper protection), and the wind will blow a fine spray a long way from the target.

LD50 figures only measure acute poisoning, and tell you nothing else about the substance. Common salt, sodium chloride (NaCl), has an LD50 figure of 3,000 mg/kg for rats, which might mean that for a human weighing 70 kg, 200 grams (say half a pound) of salt *could* be fatal. But, of course, no one thinks of salt as a poison (though some dieticians recently have worried about it) and no one would think of trying to eat that much of it. Even if you did, it would be simple enough, from a medical point of view, to flush it out, with no long-term ill effect.

The acute toxicity of captan, a fungicide, is actually *lower* than common salt, the LD50 for rats being 9,000 mg/kg. But its suspected long-term effects have caused it to be withdrawn in West Germany because it is a suspected teratogen and mutagen. A teratogen causes birth defects; a mutagen disrupts genetic information and causes hereditary defects. The problem with finding out long-term effects of a substance is obvious: it takes a long time. New pesticides may be tested over a period of seven years, but carcinogens may not show up as such for much longer, and it is hard to prove a causal link between the pesticide and the cancer.

It is estimated by the Environmental Protection Agency, an American government department, that 30 per cent of insecticides, 60 per cent of herbicides and 90 per cent of fungicides *could* cause tumours. This estimate is based on long-term exposure of rats to large amounts of chemicals.

Consider asbestos by way of comparison. Used in large amounts for many years for all manner of industrial and domestic purposes, and although an entirely *natural* substance, it is now revealed as carcinogenic. It is a very stable substance: one particle inhaled will remain in the lung indefinitely and the body has no way of getting rid of it. Fortunately, even the most persistent pesticides break down eventually, so the people most likely to be in danger will be those constantly exposed to them — farm workers, for example. A gardener occasionally exposed to a pesticide suspected of being a carcinogen is unlikely to be in any danger, any more than someone who goes into a smoke-filled pub occasionally and gets a short exposure of nicotine.

Another obvious problem with testing products on rats is that, although they may resemble humans for many purposes, they are not humans and their reactions may differ. The most notorious case is that of thalidomide, the drug prescribed for pregnant women, which led to many tragically deformed babies. No doubt the product had been exhaustively tested on various animals, with no adverse effects.

When is a substance toxic, when is it

merely harmful, when is it safe? We all know the benefits and dangers of aspirin, which has an LD50 for rats of 1,200 mg/kg. The sixteenth-century alchemist Paracelsus put it neatly: 'The poison is the dose'. This is true of a huge range of substances. The vital trace elements required by plants and animals, such as copper, zinc, manganese and boron, are poisons when present in large quantities, and all of these are incorporated in various pesticide compounds. Nitrates and phosphates in excess are serious pollutants — in fact people reading only the newspapers might believe that nitrates were only poisons, rather than an essential plant nutrient.

However, an arbitrary definition of a 'poison' might be anything lethal at under 150 mg/kg and, perhaps, equally arbitrarily, anything that requires more than 2,000 mg/kg to kill could be called 'safe'. By this definition, there are hardly any chemicals available to the amateur that are 'poisonous', but they include paraquat, gamma HCH (lindane), methiocarb, dichlorvos, bendiocarb and pirimicarb and concentrated forms of derris — but the formulations available to the gardener are so dilute that even these are not very poisonous.

Apart from the risks of acute toxicity, and suspected long-term effects like cancer, pesticides may also be irritants to eyes, nose, skin or lungs. Different people have different degrees of sensitivity to irritants. Some of the worst are common in nature — pollen and fungus spores — which may cause irritation and hay fever and asthma in some people but not in others. Most pesticides are irritant to a degree, including those approved by organic standards, such as copper, derris, potassium permanganate, pyrethrum and sulphur. If people are repeatedly exposed to an irritant they may become 'permanently sensitized' and, after that, very small amounts may trigger an allergic reation.

If used as prescribed by the manufacturers — properly diluted, avoiding breathing in or touching the spray — the pesticides available to gardeners are probably reasonably harmless to us, which is, of course, what the manufacturers keep telling us. But the toxicity of pesticides to us is only half of the picture. Their effect on other forms of life is the other half of the issue. Fungicides may damage plants, herbicides may harm insects, and so on. Insecticides are generally agreed to be the biggest problem since they almost always damage all manner of beneficial insects, such as bees and pest predators, such as ladybirds, lacewings and hoverflies, as well as countless apparently insignificant creatures. A large number of pesticides of all types are harmful to earthworms — some, of course, are designed to be so. Their effect on soil micro-organisms is largely a matter of speculation. Because they are so small, their numbers and variety so enormous, pesticides will obviously affect them even if it is not known exactly how. Pests also become resistant to pesticides — a problem we will look into later.

But perhaps the most serious damage to the environment is not due directly to the toxicity of pesticides themselves, but to the way in which they, and the agricultural methods that go with them, transform the countryside. Large fields with no hedges and single crops with all weeds eliminated are simply not much of a habitat for other forms of life. The insects and birds have nothing to feed on — except those very species that feed on that crop, i.e. the pests. Meadows that once supported a huge diversity of plant species are now reduced to one or two species of grass, and the number of insect species is similarly reduced. Birds cannot live if there is nowhere for them to nest. The loss of numbers — and whole species — of wildlife is caused less by poisoning than by starvation!

The individual gardener cannot change agricultural methods, so it is important that wildlife should be encouraged in the garden

— best of all, have an area of genuine wilderness — rather than to worry about the safety of using a little hormone rooting powder (containing thiram or captan fungicide, both 'suspected' carcinogens) to get cuttings going.

# Insecticides

Let us look at the different types of pesticide individually in more detail, starting with *insecticides*. The 'pests' are insects that eat cultivated plants, harm or inconvenience people. The 'non-pests' are predators of pests, pollinators (such as bees) and producers of useful materials (bees again). The rest may not be directly important to us, but they are all part of the chain, and if in any doubt must be considered desirable rather than otherwise. Included with 'insects' are many other small animals that are not actually insects: millipedes, centipedes, eelworms and mites, which are important both as pests *and* as predators, and earthworms which are quite unlike insects but very susceptible to a number of pesticides.

How do they work? In a variety of ways, often several ways in combination.

*Contact poisons* work by penetrating the body surface or by the insect walking over a surface with insecticide on it.

*Stomach poisons* work when the insect eats the leaf with pesticide on it.

*Fumigants.* Some insecticides are sufficiently volatile to produce a toxic vapour which gets into the insect.

*Systemic.* These are absorbed into the sap stream (phloem) of plants and so sap-sucking insects, such as aphids and scale-insects, are the target.

Insecticides may be further classified as 'specific' (or selective) in action, or as 'broad spectrum'. Pirimicarb is fairly selective against aphids; gamma HCH is a broad-spectrum insecticide and will harm most insects. The problem with broad-spectrum insecticides is that they kill both pest and predator (as well as the innocent bystanders). The surviving pests then repopulate, but with few predators to control them. Generally, predators are *larger* creatures than their prey; larger creatures tend to have a longer life cycle than smaller ones, which means they take *longer* to recover from any depletion of population than their prey, and this means that the pest becomes more of a problem than it was before. This is called *resurgence*.

The ideal insecticide is one that kills only the pest and not the predator. But even this could be problematic: if the pest is killed, the predator also starves, and the surviving pests (there are *always* a few) repopulate faster than the predator, leading *again* to the resurgence problem.

It costs in the region of £15 million to develop a new pesticide. Only one in ten thousand of those discovered and tested is used. Toxicity tests last five years or more, during which time no profit is made. No wonder pesticides are expensive. When a new product *does* reach the market, the manufacturers are anxious to sell as much of it as possible to cover their costs and make a profit. It is understandable, therefore, that there is more profit in broad-spectrum pesticides than in selective ones.

I mentioned the different types of insecticide in Chapter 2. The *organochlorines* DDT, aldrin, gamma HCH, chlordane — are on their way out. Their notorious persistence, which was originally their selling point, is now accepted as a disadvantage. However, they are still in use in large quantities, especially in the Third World, and gamma HCH (lindane) is still available to amateurs in this country. It is also a standard ingredient in timber-treatment products where its persistence is an obvious advantage to any firm wanting to give a 25-year guarantee against woodworm!

Organochlorines generally act by contact, ingestion and sometimes by vapour action. They are all *non*-systemic. Toxicity to humans varies, but if somehow you should get a lethal dose, there is no remedy.

*Organophosphates* vary a great deal in persistence, toxicity and selectivity, and some, such as dimethoate, are systemic as well as working by contact or vapour action. It is hard to generalize with them. Parathion is quite deadly, whereas malathion — available to the amateur — is reasonably safe. Their names are sufficiently similar to give malathion the same deadly reputation as parathion. They are all nerve poisons, for mammals as well as insects, and operate by inhibiting the enzyme cholinesterase — hence they are also known as 'anti-cholinesterase compounds'. In the unlikely event of a lethal dose, atropine sulphate and pralidoxim are antidotes. Organophosphates available to the gardener include dichlorvos, malathion, fenitrothion, bromophos, dimethoate, phoxim, pirimiphos-methyl and chlorpyriphos.

*Carbamates* are also cholinesterase inhibitors and in the unlikely event of poisoning, atropine sulphate is also the antidote (but not pralidoxim). There are fewer of these than organophosphates, but they likewise vary in power and hazardousness. Carbaryl is the best known and safest, available for amateur use. The Union Carbide factory that blew up in Bhopal causing many deaths and many more serious and long-term injuries was a carbaryl factory but it was not carbaryl that killed people, but the chemicals involved in its manufacture. Other carbamates available to amateurs are pirimicarb (very poisonous but useful because it is a specific aphicide) and bendiocarb (extremely poisonous, LD50 as low as 35 mg/kg, but only available to gardeners very heavily diluted).

Natural pyrethrum along with derris and nicotine were the most common insecticides in the past. Pyrethrum, a flower of the chrysanthemum family, is a broad-spectrum contact insecticide, moderately toxic to mammals. It breaks down *very* rapidly in sunlight or air — this is generally considered an advantage. Synthetic pyrethroids ('pyrethrum-like') are, as their name suggests, chemically related to pyrethrum, but some last considerably longer. Some are more, some are less toxic to humans than natural pyrethrum. The synthetic pyrethroids operate by contact and, like natural pyrethrum, generally have a rapid 'knock-down' effect. Insects might recover from a small dose after this initial knock-down, but if formulated with a little of another insecticide, this usually finishes them off. If pyrethroids are used on their own, bees may survive small doses for this reason. They are commonly used in household fly-sprays, as well as for controlling many other pests.

Synthetic pyrethroids include allethrin, permethrin, resmethrin and tetramethrin, and they are often used with 'synergists', such as piperonyl butoxide, which increases their power against insects without apparently increasing their toxicity to us. Permethrin is the only one available to amateurs that is at all persistent, and it breaks down rapidly in soil.

Derris, or rotenone, is an effective fish poison. Being a natural plant extract, the proportion of active ingredient and the toxicity varies enormously. The strongest has an LD50 of only 50 — well into the 'poisonous' area — and the weakest is ten times less toxic!

Nicotine, until recently accepted by organic gardeners, is now banned for amateur use. Since it is so poisonous, why did organic gardeners approve it? Partly because it is 'natural', and the fact that it is non-persistent and, although a very powerful poison, it spares some useful predators, such as ladybirds and hoverfly larvae.

Soap sprays have been around a long time — at least 150 years. Now that it is illegal to make your own, Koppert and Safers can sell a lot more of their registered products. The active ingredient is described technically as 'fatty acids'. There are many different 'fatty acids', and commercial manufacturers naturally want us to think their combinations are best — which may well be so, as they have spent a great deal of time and money trying different soaps at different concentrations on different plants.

Soap works quite well against aphids, scale, mites, whiteflies and some other pests, particularly on soft-bodied insects. It probably works by dissolving the waxy coating on insects' bodies and then disrupting their osmotic balance. It is virtually completely safe to us, but soap will sting, of course, if it gets in your eye (it upsets the osmotic balance of your eyeball too, but fortunately you are millions of times bigger than an aphid). The main problem is phytotoxicity: depending on the dosage, species and vigour of the plant. Soap is a wetting agent, or 'surfactant', and many formulations of more toxic chemicals contain surfactants to improve their efficacy.

Finally, Bacillus thuringiensis. This is really a biological control, but since it is available in a packet and is applied as a spray for practical purposes, it is like a chemical insecticide (and indeed, is often mixed with pyrethrum for luck). It is actually a bacterium which is effective mainly against butterfly caterpillars, so it is good for dealing with caterpillars on cabbages. It works because the bacterium releases chemical toxins and these kill the caterpillar. It does not survive in the long term and so it has to be re-applied if necessary. It is completely selective and does not cause any significant harm to anything else. The subject of biological control will be looked at in Chapter 7.

The problem of *resistance* occurs with fungicides and herbicides also, but perhaps is most crucial with insecticides. It is not a new problem. The first recorded case involved a scale insect resistant to hydrogen cyanide about 90 years ago. But the problem has been accelerating over the last 20 years in direct proportion to the increase in the use of pesticides. It is caused by using the same chemical against the same pest over a long period. The same problem is encountered with drugs when human disease organisms acquire a resistance to antibiotics. It is a wonderful example of evolutionary adaptation, which enables all kinds of living organisms to survive in the face of threats to their existence. Some weeds have developed resistance to weedkillers, and there is a serious problem with systemic fungicides (such as benomyl).

There are various ways that insects acquire resistance. They may find a way to chemically alter the toxin — specific enzymes appear which make the necessary chemical changes. They may become 'thicker-skinned' with either the outer body surface or the gut wall becoming less permeable to the poison. Or, they may somehow learn to avoid poisoned surfaces, and thus simply not come into contact with them.

There is no limit to the types of chemical to which a pest can become resistant and there is no reason why pests should not become resistant to the poisons used by organic gardeners. Indeed, a Soil Association report recently admitted that substantial resistance to pyrethrum has built up in some parts of the world and in a range of insect pests.

Complex organic molecules which happen to be poisonous can be *very* similar to others which are not, and the ability of pests to make subtle changes to de-toxify them is, as mentioned above, one of the ways pests develop resistance. The advantage of the simple inorganic pesticides is that this cannot happen — the disadvantages being that they are more toxic and very persistent.

# Fungicides

Plants come under attack from various organisms, including viruses and bacteria. Viruses are not controllable with chemicals — plants susceptible to virus disease, such as raspberries, are best bought as guaranteed virus-free stock, and any that are later infected simply have to be destroyed. Bacteria are also difficult to control in practice — other than by the sterilants or disinfectants which are used to clean up greenhouses or to sterilize soils, and these are generally poisonous to plants as well.

However, fungi, the other main type of plant 'pathogen', are susceptible to subtler means of control. As with insecticides, the requirement is for something that will kill the fungus without harming the plant. Since plants are biologically similar to fungi, phytotoxicity is one of the main problems with them, and most of the traditional fungicides, such as sulphur, mercury and copper, have this drawback. Whatever criticisms we may have of modern fungicides, most have at least overcome this problem.

Fungicides are classified as 'protectant' or 'curative' or both, and may or may not be systemic as well.

A protectant fungicide, as the name suggests, will not cure a plant that is already infected, but will protect a healthy plant from attack. Relatively few fungicides have a genuine curative effect. It is hard to kill an established fungus disease without killing the plant too, because, as just stated, their individual cells are not dissimilar.

Systemic protectant fungicides started with benomyl (Benlate) and others available to the gardener include carbendazim, thiabendazole and thiophanate-methyl. These four also have a broad-spectrum activity. Systemic fungicides were regarded as an amazing breakthrough and, of course, have been over-used, with their natural consequence: resistance. Farmers now have to change their fungicide frequently to keep the fungi on the hop.

A particular advantage of systemic fungicides — and insecticides — is that the underside of the leaf is where many fungi and insects take a hold. The underside of the leaf is the area least accessible to pesticides because dusts simply fall off, and sprays have to be directed upwards from underneath. A systemic pesticide, once in the sap, will reach all of the plant's surfaces.

The non-systemic fungicides, such as the di-thiocarbamates, developed before the systemic, are still used in large quantities. Despite their wide use and broad-spectrum activity, resistance problems have not been encountered.

The only fungicides approved by organic standards are copper and sulphur. Sulphur has a specific action against powdery mildews and is generally not phytotoxic except to a few 'sulphur-shy' species. Like many traditional pesticides, it has not been investigated in the way that new ones have. It is generally regarded as 'relatively non-toxic', although fairly persistent. Because of sulphur's main use as a fungicide, it has often been forgotten that it is an insecticide and acaricide too, and there have been many cases of increase in pests — especially fruit tree spider mite in orchards — due to the loss of predators after frequent use of sulphur.

Bordeaux mixture, a combination of copper sulphate and lime, was traditionally mixed 'on site' in a tank. Copper sulphate is a very corrosive material — it was used originally as a weed killer — and the addition of lime, or other alkali, neutralizes the acidity and makes it less harmful to plants. *Real* Bordeaux mixture works best when freshly mixed, but it is no longer permitted to make your own, because of the very hazardous nature of copper sulphate.

The copper fungicides available to the

amateur are wettable powders or colloidal suspensions and are not really Bordeaux mixture as such, but the copper in them is the active ingredient. Copper oxychloride and cuprous oxide are other copper fungicides. Various alkalis have been combined with copper sulphate including ammonium carbonate, sodium carbonate (washing soda) and sodium bicarbonate; the last of these, which people take for acid indigestion, has recently been investigated as a fungicide in its own right.

How do fungicides work? Fungi are not like insects. Apart from honey-fungus, which attacks trees and shrubs whose fruiting body looks like a toadstool, most of the fungi that are plant pests are very small, and their spores are always microscopic.

Non-systemic fungicides are mainly general cell poisons — to both plant and fungus — but they kill the pest only, because they do not penetrate the cuticle (waxy surface) of the leaf. However, systemic fungicides must be able to enter the plant without killing it. Benomyl, thiophanate methyl and thiabendazole all work by disrupting DNA (genetic material) production. When plants or fungi (or people) are actively growing, there is a great deal of cell-division and DNA synthesis going on. But most parts of a plant — other than the meristem (or growing tip) — are *not* actively growing, whereas the invading fungi are growing very rapidly. For this reason they get knocked out far more rapidly than the plant. It is a very clever mechanism. A substance that disrupts DNA production is, by definition, a mutagen, and mutagens are also carcinogens. These are both words with horrendous associations.

Many substances, natural or artificial, are carcinogens. There was even a pop-song called 'Everything gives you cancer'. Cabbage, comfrey, coltsfoot, low-fat diets, bracken, sassafras, the list continues. Ultraviolet light, which is the only part of the sunlight spectrum that enables us to manufacture vitamin D, is also carcinogenic, if taken in excess. James Lovelock, the environmental scientist famous for his 'Gaia' theory which suggests that the world is a living organism itself, quotes in *The Ages of Gaia* an interesting, and somehow reassuring, theory. Oxygen is a mutagen and carcinogen:

> Breathing oxygen may be what sets a limit to the life span of most animals, but not breathing it is even more rapidly lethal. There is a right level of oxygen, namely 21 per cent; more or less than this can be harmful. To set a level of zero for oxygen in the interest of preventing cancer would be most unwise.

Mutagens and carcinogens aside, systemic fungicides are fairly safe as pesticides go. The LD50 for benomyl is 10,000 mg/kg — three times less poisonous than common salt — with thiabendazole at 3,300 — about the same as salt. You would be much more likely to feel ill after a lungful of Bordeaux mixture or sulphur than with a lungful of systemic fungicide. But there is no doubt that calomel, mercurous chloride, should be avoided. It is very poisonous to most forms of life and simply should not be spread around. As it is, its use is restricted to soil for controlling brassica clubroot and onion white rot.

A final, important point about fungicides: even though some fungicides do have a 'curative' effect, if you wait until a fungus is visibly established on a plant it will be much harder to deal with. It is therefore understandable that people use fungicides preventatively, when there might be no visible need to do so. You may condemn the use of fungicides, but if you do use them, they are much more effective if applied preventatively. This contrasts with insecticides or herbicides where there is much less justification for spraying against a problem that you do not yet have!

# Herbicides

Weeds are the most easily detectable garden pests — you can't miss them! Consequently they are the easiest to remove manually: you pull them up, hoe them off, dig them out. But they need the most constant vigilance because they really will take over your garden and ruin it if not kept in check.

Apart from the ploughing once a year, farmers in the developed world use herbicides almost exclusively for weed control. You do not see farmers out in the fields with a hoe, but I have seen farmers' wives (!) out on cattle-grazing areas pulling up ragwort by hand. Ragwort, which looks like a tall yellow daisy, is poisonous to cattle. Quite sensibly they avoid it, but if it is mixed with hay they can not do so. So, the ragwort grows to maturity, shunned by cattle, it flowers, sets seeds, and rapidly spreads. One chalk downland hill that I have known for many years was sprayed *once* with combined selective herbicide and nitrogen fertilizer. There was uproar in the village, and the farmer did not do it again. But it temporarily 'controlled' most of the attractive 'weeds' — campanula, scabious, orchids and many others, and the grass grew greener and longer. But it did not make a lot of difference to the rather more resilient ragwort which, having less competition from the other weeds, subsequently did rather better. The hillside has almost recovered now, though it is not quite the same as it was and the rarer species of orchids have not returned. But now the farmer's wife pulls up the ragwort!

This kind of outrage is the stuff of good environmentalist journalism, but let us go to the other extreme. What harm can it do to put a total weedkiller on a garden path or patio? It saves a lot of time and effort, and since nothing else is growing there, it can do no harm. Trying to dig bits of grass and dandelion from between paving slabs is a boring, backbreaking job which has to be frequently repeated — one application of a modern path weedkiller will do the trick for a season.

Classification of herbicides is complex. Herbicides are either selective or total, contact or translocated (which means the same as 'systemic' — it gets into the plant's sap) or residual (that is, soil-acting as opposed to foliar-acting) or some combination of these! Some are also described as 'pre-emergent' or 'post-emergent', i.e., applied *before* the crop appears above ground level or *after*.

Sodium chlorate was once the favourite total weedkiller. The disadvantages are that it is explosive (modern products contain a fire-suppressant) and tends to spread into other areas where desirable plants are growing. It also persists in the soil for about six months. It is a 'residual' herbicide.

Paraquat and diquat are other well-known contact total weedkillers. They work by contact with the leaves and that part only is destroyed. Therefore, established, perennial weeds like ground elder or convolvulus will not be seriously affected. Paraquat is 'soil-inactivated', which means that it is strongly adsorbed immediately on to clay particles in the soil (see Chapter 4). There is considerable argument about the ultimate fate of paraquat, but if soil contains no clay, it cannot be 'inactivated'. If it were used on a very peaty piece of the garden, perhaps where rhododendrons are growing, it *might* remain active for some time.

Glyphosate (Tumbleweed) is a very popular total weedkiller. It is translocated into the whole plant, and therefore can kill deep-rooted perennials. But even this may need several applications to get rid of some of the worst weeds. It is very 'safe' (LD50 5,600 mg/kg).

Ammonium sulphamate (Amcide) used to be the organic gardener's exception to the rules. It is a total herbicide used commercially for killing tree stumps. It breaks down within three weeks to become ammonium sulphate, the ordinary nitrogen fertilizer. Why organic gardeners should have singled out this one as acceptable is a mystery. Not only is it a weedkiller, but it also ends up as a chemical fertilizer! Now, however, it is excluded with all the others, though many organic gardeners still use it.

The best known of the 'translocated' herbicides are of the 'hormone' type. Since it was discovered that overdoses of auxin, the natural plant hormone, arrested plant growth rather than stimulated it, a range of synthetic auxins have been developed as weedkillers. The special feature of these is that they are specific in action against broad-leaved weeds and do not harm grasses, which include cereal crops as well as lawns. To this day, despite masses of research, no one knows *why* these herbicides do not harm grasses.

Of these herbicides, the best known are: 2, 4-D; 2, 4, 5-T; MCPA, and Mecoprop — all available to gardeners except 2, 4, 5-T, which, although still registered for amateur use, is no longer manufactured as a garden product in this country. The most infamous of weedkillers, 2, 4, 5-T, is particularly useful against woody perennial weeds; it is marketed as a 'brushwood' killer. Its infamy derives from its use in Vietnam, under the trade name 'Agent Orange'. The intention was to defoliate the entire countryside so that communist guerillas would become visible and so attackable. It was also badly contaminated with TCDD, or dioxin, which had far *worse* effects on the population than the defoliation of their forests. The 2, 4, 5-T now manufactured contains negligible amounts of dioxin, but it is still a fairly poisonous substance and is regarded by scientists as 'recalcitrant' — a nice word meaning very resistant to degradation by micro-organisms.

The whole question of what happens to pesticides in general (not just weedkillers) in the soil is hard to approach; what research there has been has been done in laboratories, of course, and field conditions are bound to vary enormously. There is concern that in some cases the products of the breakdown may be more persistent or dangerous than the originals.

Some herbicides are selective *against* grasses rather than in favour of them, but generally less reliable as they tend to damage broad-leaved plants as well. Alloxydim-sodium is one of the best of these and controls perennial grasses including common couch quite well, whereas aminotriazole (amitrole), although particularly effective against grasses, will kill other perennials too, and is consequently a common ingredient in path weedkillers (e.g. ICI Pathclear).

Residual herbicides are soil-acting rather than foliar, and remain in the soil, as their name implies, for a long time (a year, more or less). Simazine, typically, is used under trees and shrubs and fruit bushes and controls any weeds germinating in the area, but it can be used in asparagus beds too as the fat shoots are strong enough and quick enough to escape any damage.

How do they work? The hormone type weedkillers overstimulate the plant's metabolism; some, like paraquat, interrupt photosynthesis, some disrupt respiration, and others, such as propham and chlorpropham, disrupt normal cell division. (These last two are no longer available to the amateur.) Generally, herbicides are less toxic to humans than insecticides; inevitably many are suspected carcinogens, mutagens or teratogens. Even 2, 4-D, considered for years as very safe, has recently come under suspicion of causing a cancer (non-Hodgkin's lymphoma).

One thing we do not have to worry about with herbicides, however, is their residue on food, since we do not eat weeds, and even where crops are sprayed with herbicides, this is normally at an early stage, so the poison does not get onto the part we eat.

Herbicides have possibly transformed the landscape more than any other pesticide. Reducing the variety of plants growing has reduced the variety of insects and birds. It is well known that Buddleia and Sedum spectabile attract butterflies to the garden, but the larvae of the species of butterfly that are

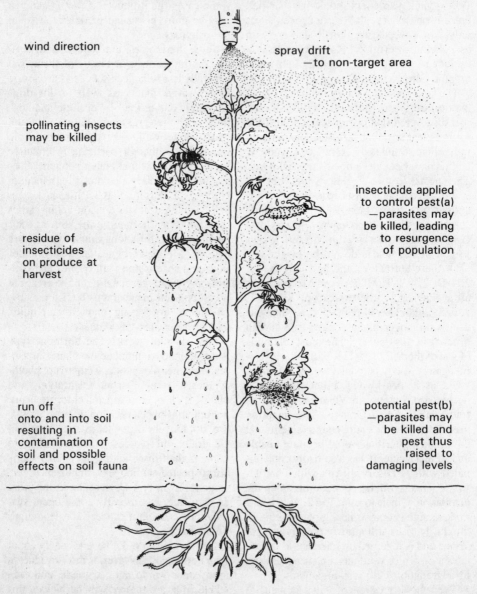

wind direction

spray drift
—to non-target area

pollinating insects
may be killed

insecticide applied
to control pest(a)
—parasites may
be killed, leading
to resurgence
of population

residue of
insecticides
on produce at
harvest

run off
onto and into soil
resulting in
contamination of
soil and possible
effects on soil fauna

potential pest(b)
—parasites may
be killed and
pest thus
raised to
damaging levels

Fig 12: the disadvantages of insecticides

around at buddleia flowering time (such as tortoiseshells, red admirals and peacocks) feed on stinging nettles. So no buddleia bush is going to attract tortoiseshell butterflies unless nettles are also growing nearby. This is however, a rather crude illustration of the problem. The butterflies mentioned *are* still common because there is not really any shortage of nettles, but the fact is that most insect larvae are very particular about what they feed on, and their foods plants are mostly 'weeds' — the exceptions being those insects that are crop pests, such as the cabbage white butterfly.

# Miscellaneous

Under this heading we have molluscicides, vertebrate controls and timber treatments.

*Molluscicides* kill slugs and snails. Most gardeners use poison baits, the active ingredient of which is metaldehyde. Sometimes slugs and snails recover from this and live to try again. Methiocarb is less popular but more poisonous. Organic gardeners use aluminium sulphate, which was mentioned earlier in the book. It is described as 'non-poisonous', but how can it be if it kills slugs and also caused a lot of sickness when accidentally dumped into the Cornish water supply? It does not pose any threat to frogs, hedgehogs, birds or pets, which the other two might, but its efficacy as a slug killer is also disputed; used in quantity, it will not do your soil any good.

*Vertebrate controls* are a polite term for rat and mouse poisons. There is not much to be said about these, except that anything poisonous to rats and mice is going to be poisonous also to humans. Also under this heading are 'mole smokes', which are supposed to deter rather than kill the animals. Until recently, mole smokes contained lindane and tecnazene — insecticide and fungicide respectively — which gives an indication of how unpleasant they must be, but the only substance now found in amateur mole smokes is sulphur (the organic gardener's favourite fungicide). Finally, there are cat and dog repellants, usually containing pepper.

*Timber treatments* As a precondition of your mortgage your house may well have had timber treatment, which will have been a combination of insecticide and fungicide. For a 20- or 25-years guarantee to be given, fairly hefty chemicals have to be used — with the emphasis on persistence. There is an enormous number of products in use, with a variety of active ingredients. The issues involved in house-timber treatments are outside the scope of this book, but you will also encounter some of these when buying a timber preservative for your greenhouse, shed or fencing. They are nearly all poisonous to plants, and since they obviously contain persistent chemicals, will remain so. If plants are likely to come into contact with your fence, make sure you use a preservative with low phytotoxicity, such as Cuprinol Green.

# Conclusion

Even if we only consider those available to the amateur, the variety of pesticides is fairly mindboggling. What conclusions can we draw? No doubt a few, including some organic ones, are dangerous, and these are only available to amateurs in very unconcentrated formulations. No doubt many are fairly safe, though most can have adverse effects on the environment. But all of them were developed for commercial use and have to a degree been foisted on the amateur market. Why should we want to treat our gardens in the way that farmers treat farms? (If only farmers could treat their farms like gardens!)

Forget the dangers of pesticides for a moment and ask if they are necessary. The most likely answer will be, yes, occasionally, but not very often. Many of the problems of an average garden can be spotted by one pair of eyes and sorted out with one pair of hands. Where this is not possible, either some kind of chemical control will be required, or the plant simply not grown. A friend of mine took this option to the extreme: she had a fine peach tree, which even yielded some fruit, but cut it down rather than have to spray twice a year with fungicide against leaf curl disease.

If it comes to the last resort, and the decision is made to spray, the choice generally seems to be: either a single, or relatively few, good blasts with something really effective, or the repeated use of something less effective. The 'green' gardener who wants effective pest control might end up doing more spraying than his 'chemical' neighbour! There is no simple, generalized way out of this dilemma, but what should be avoided, at least, is the blanket use of pesticides whether they are necessary or not: it is pointless, wasteful and potentially harmful in all the ways described in this chapter.

A further reason for not using pesticides is simply their cost. They are expensive even to the farmer, who buys in bulk and who can offset their cost against his tax. But to the amateur buying them in small quantities their price is proportionately many times higher. This further encourages people to buy broad-spectrum chemicals and those 'multi' products that contain fertilizer, fungicide and insecticide together. These may be useful if, for instance, your roses need feeding and are infested with aphids as well as mildew and blackspot. But there is no doubt that many people use them when only *one* treatment is required. Roses then get sprayed with insecticide when they have only mildew, or fungicide when they have only aphids, or are dosed with both when all they needed was a feed.

Some of the means that organic gardeners use to control pests without pesticides are mentioned in Chapter 7.

*See the tables on pp. 82-102 for active ingredients of pesticides and for a selection of proprietary products, including the active ingredient they contain.*

# 6
# *Manures and composts*

$M$atter is matter, neither noble nor vile, infinitely transformable, and its proximate origin is of no importance whatsoever. Nitrogen is nitrogen, it passes miraculously from the air into plants, from these into animals, and from animals to us; when its function in our body is exhausted, we eliminate it, but it still remains nitrogen, aseptic, innocent.

Primo Levi (*The Periodic Table*) wrote this in the context of trying, shortly after the war when materials were scarce, to extract a dye for making kissproof lipstick from chicken manure! He failed, but this quotation illustrates rather eloquently the fact that the nitrogen plants need is the same whether it comes from the Haber process (see Chapter 2, page 21) or from poultry manure. Nicholas Ridley, a former Environment Secretary, put it more directly but less elegantly: 'What comes out of the back end of a cow is as potent a source of nitrogen as any chemical fertilizer.' What he did not say was that what comes from the back end of a cow, if mixed with straw and allowed to rot a little, improves the soil in a way that no chemical fertilizer can. Which brings us to manures, as well as composts and soil-conditioners.

Fertilizers — both organic and inorganic — have been discussed in Chapter 4. What distinguishes manures and composts from fertilizers is their bulkiness. Their nutrient content and value in the garden vary enormously.

## Soil conditioners

Soil conditioners are generally not regarded as sources of plant food (though they contain some that is slowly released as they break down) but as materials for increasing the organic content of soil, or as a mulch on its surface. Peat is the most commonly used. The best, and the one normally available, is moss (rather than sedge) peat. It is found in Ireland and the West of Scotland, also in the Pennines, on acidic rocks, where the acidic litter from heather and sphagnum moss builds up slowly in continuous wet and therefore anaerobic (airless) conditions. The process is comparable with the 'tanning' of leather: instead of rotting away, it is chemically altered and preserved. It is a limited resource and is being used up far faster than it is being created. Being fairly acidic, it can help neutralize alkaline soils, where it breaks down very quickly. It is also very useful for increasing the acidity of soils where rhododendrons and other acid lovers, such as heather, are grown.

*Peat* is a type of humus — soil scientists call it 'mor humus' as opposed to 'mull humus' — which is normally produced when vegetable matter decays. The differences are striking. Mull humus is much less acid, is full of plant nutrients and has a very fine structure so that it is sticky and will hold on to nutrients (see Chapter 4). Peat is low in plant nutrients, has a very loose structure and its capacity to hold water, and nutrients in solution, is like that of a sponge.

*Leaf mould* is an excellent soil conditioner, but it cannot generally be bought, it has to be made. When leaves fall from decaying trees in autumn, most of the mobile ions, such as nitrogen (N), phosphorus (P) and potassium (K), have migrated back down to the roots to be stored over winter. What is left in an autumn leaf if mostly cellulose, lignins and calcium — woody stuff. Leaf mould is less acid than peat and contains slightly more potassium and nitrogen, but otherwise

serves a similar purpose. Making a leaf-mould heap is quite different from making compost — the heap does not heat up and the process takes a long time, at least a year. Beech and oak leaves have the reputation of being the best, but there is no reason why other leaves should not be just as good. If you have a large garden with a lot of trees you should gather your own supply (remember that you are depriving your woodland of its natural supply of humus!), otherwise leaves have to be acquired from somewhere else, which is easier said than done. But if leaves are available, you simply put them in a large bin made of posts driven into the ground, with wire-mesh in between, and tread them down a bit.

*Forest waste* is another commercially available soil conditioner. It is a mixture of shredded bark and woodchips, and it must be fully composted if it is to be dug in, otherwise the process of decomposition will temporarily rob the soil of nitrogen. Generally, like leaf mould, it is applied as a mulch in a thick layer on the soil surface to suppress weeds and conserve moisture. It will gradually be incorporated into the soil by earthworms and other soil creatures.

# Potting composts

As mentioned in the Introduction, there are two basic types of potting composts: soil-based and soil-less. Soil-less composts — based on peat — now dominate the commercial and amateur market for two reasons at least. First, peat is much lighter than soil so transport and handling are a lot cheaper and easier. Second, the 'soil' or 'loam' ingredient of the John Innes type of compost is supposed to be derived from rotted turf, but there just is not enough spare turf around to be rotted for the expanding market, and the 'loam' content can be a bit iffy as a result. John Innes composts come in several grades:

cuttings, seed, No. 1, No. 2 and No. 3 — with varying proportions of sand, peat and loam, and increasing amounts of J.I. base fertilizer (a balanced mixture of hoof and horn, superphosphate and potassium sulphate with an overall analysis of 13-18-24), ranging from none in 'cuttings' and 'seed' grades to a lot in No. 3.

Manufacturers are not obliged to state the precise composition of composts. There are recommendations given by the Glasshouse Crops Research Institute for the composition of soil-less seed and potting composts, similar to those of the John Innes types, but without the loam, and with added lime and trace elements. Most of the compost sold now is 'general purpose'. The idea behind graded composts is that cuttings and seedlings not only do not *need* large supplies of fertilizers, but also cannot cope with them: a strong solution around their newly developing roots will upset their osmotic balance and stop them developing properly. So a multipurpose compost must contain the same, or very little more nutrient than the old 'seed' and 'cuttings' composts. This simply means that they need additional fertilizer sooner if used for potting established plants.

The Ministry of Agriculture, Fisheries and Food (MAFF) recently conducted tests, at the request of Fisons who make 'Levington' composts, to compare various brands of general-purpose composts and also John Innes No. 1 and No. 2. 'Levington' came out on top, which is fair enough, but the John Innes types came out last on the list, which is *not* fair, because they are not supposed to be general-purpose composts, and are certainy not designed for seed sowing.

There are other potting composts created for the 'organic' market that contain composted cow manures as an alternative to the loam in J.I. composts, and some with composted forest waste instead of peat, along with rock phosphate instead of superphosphate and rock potash instead of potassium sulphate. As yet organic standards do not insist on this type of material for propagating plants, but no doubt they soon will.

## Other composts

Next we come to the other type of *compost*. Composting is a process that breaks down fresh organic matter into a brown, crumbly stuff that looks rather like nice soil. It is an accelerated version of what happens naturally to plant residues. The essence of the process is that it is aerobic — airy. There are many books devoted to compost, and most gardening books have a lengthy mention of it — usually with a picture of a wooden structure about one metre high and deep and two metres wide, divided into two compartments: one for the heap that is being made, the other for maturing the heap that is finished. It is a far from boring topic, but there are so many favourite ways of doing it that I shall not add my own. You can even build your own compost container from bales of straw, though strict organic gardeners would have to be certain there were no pesticide residues in the straw. The most important thing, whatever your design, is to make sure air can get in at the bottom: putting wire mesh over a few bricks is a good idea.

The principle is this: layers of garden or kitchen waste (*not* meat, take-away leftovers or fat; vegetable only or you will get a bad smell and/or rats) are interspersed with layers of something rich in nitrogen: ammonium sulphate; dried blood or animal manure, with or without layers of lime to counteract acidity. Fungi and bacteria feed on these materials, and a supply of oxygen is necessary for them. Sometimes heaps are turned to aerate them, or poles stuck in to provide extra air holes. If all goes well, it gets very hot (up to 70°C) and the mixture begins to rot very quickly, and in the process weed seeds, pathogens and even perennial weed roots are killed. The compost can be used after the hot part of the fermentation when it will be still relatively coarse or it can be left to mature further.

Most people do not get ideal results from composting, but the end product is always worth having. Unless you are certain the whole heap, including the outside, will heat up well, it is best to leave out perennial weed roots. Serious composters, with large

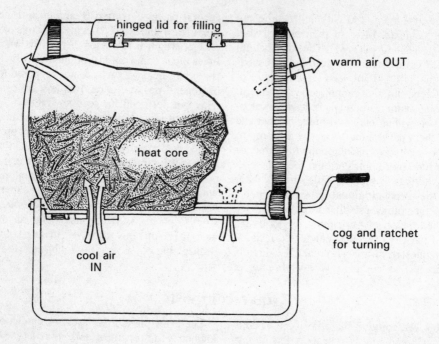

hinged lid for filling

warm air OUT

heat core

cog and ratchet
for turning

cool air
IN

Fig 13: compost tumbler

gardens or some other source of raw material, can acquire a shredder which will make cabbage stumps and even woody material useable, and a 'tumbler' — a large revolving drum which is turned every day — in which conditions are more easily controllable.

Compost can be made on a small scale — if you do not have the space or quantity of material for a large heat-generating bin — using brandling worms (Eisenia foetida). They are similar to, but smaller than, the ordinary earthworm, and if you have a compost or manure heap, there will almost certainly be some in it. Otherwise you can get them mail order from organic suppliers or from fishing suppliers — brandling worms are also used as bait.

The principle is simple: you feed the worms with kitchen waste and they turn it into compost. In practice it is more complicated because the worms are a bit fussy about their conditions: it must be warm and not too acid. A plastic dustbin with a lid is the basic requirement. Drainage holes are bored into the bottom six inches; above this a wooden board, also with drainage holes; a layer of sedge peat (not as acid as moss peat) or even shredded damp newspaper. The worms are placed on this, and then layers of vegetable waste — even some fat and meat — alternating with peat. Once it is full, it is turned occasionally with a fork, until the worms have digested it all; the compost is then removed and as many worms as possible put back, and the process started again. The worms will not be active in the winter, but as long as they do not freeze, they will survive.

# Animal manures

These manures depend on the animal. Cow manure, or farmyard manure (FYM), horse and pig, are the most commonly used. The composition naturally varies considerably, not just the proportions of nutrients and water, but most importantly, the amount of straw. As with garden compost the nitrogenous elements and the plant residues rot together to make a nice end product — a good soil conditioner and source of nutrients. In the days of 'mixed' farms where cereals were grown as well as cattle raised, farmyard manure was plentiful and useful. Cereal and cattle production is often separate now, so farmers end up with a problem of waste disposal. Cow slurry becomes an environmental pollutant instead of a useful fertilizer.

If farmyard manure is to be dug in, it is best left to rot for a year even if some nutrients are lost in the process. Raw manure will adversely affect plants in a number of ways: first, there will be a lot of free nitrogen which may 'burn' the roots of seedlings, and cause carrots or parsnips to 'fork'. When this has either been used up, washed out or volatilized into the air, there will be a lot of unrotted straw left: the soil organisms will steal what nitrogen is left to rot down that straw, leaving the growing plants with a temporary deficiency, which will have to be corrected by adding some extra fertilizer.

This is particularly important with horse or chicken manure, which is generally mixed with wood chippings. These break down even more slowly than straw and can deplete soil nitrogen for even longer. A further reason for rotting manure thoroughly is that any pesticide residues are also degraded. Persistent chemicals often found in straw include lindane, benomyl and 2, 3, 6 -TBA — which is similar to 2, 4-D, but more durable and could conceivably damage garden plants the following season.

Finally, there are the concentrated 'organic' manures. There are several of these on the market — the worst are wood chip and battery poultry manure, dried and bagged and sold as 'six times richer than farm yard manure'; the best are simply concentrated composted cow manure. Since they are concentrated, they are best treated as a fertilizer — spread at so many ounces per square yard, rather than in shovelfuls. They are also expensive — about £8 per bag compared with, say, £30 for a trailer load of unconcentrated manure, so they are not a substitute if you have anything more than a tiny garden. A further disadvantage is that being 'live' substances sealed in a plastic bag they can actually go 'off'; anaerobic bacteria can get established and produce toxins which could harm your plants, so it is best not to store them too long.

Various types of manure and fertilizers are mentioned in the A to Z, and some brands of compost are mentioned in the table of 'organic' products.

# 7
# Organic methods and new technology

If you are a commercial grower, the choice is simple: if you want to get the premium on your produce as an organic producer, you have to obey certain rules in order to get your 'Soil Association Symbol'. The rules are basically: no artificial fertilizer and no pesticides, with a few specified exceptions. (If you have animals as well as crops, similar restrictions apply and many normal veterinary treatments are outlawed as well, making it difficult to control parasites such as lice, ticks and worms in your livestock.) There is no point in following the spirit of organic growing and then using your own judgement when you encounter problems: if you do this and break the rules, you will not be able to sell your produce as 'organic'.

If you are an ordinary gardener, whether or not you swallow the 'organic' message whole is up to you; the purpose of this book is to present the issues as openly as possible. There are numerous books on all aspects of 'organic' gardening, and the techniques involved, so there is no need here to go into great detail. Not all good gardening practice is confined to 'organic' gardeners, and many of the techniques described in organic books are the same as those found anywhere else. However, here are a few general points. (You will find other useful information in the A

to Z.)

Crop rotation not only helps prevent build-up of pests specific to particular crops, but also generally improves soil fertility as each type of crop takes out different proportions of nitrogen, phosphorus and potassium and other nutrients, and plants of the pea family actually add to soil nitrogen. Potatoes are prone to eelworm which can remain dormant in the soil for years; brassicas (cabbage family) suffer from clubroot. Legumes, pota-

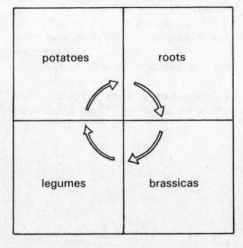

Fig 14: crop rotation

toes and brassicas can form the basis for a crop-rotation cycle, with root crops including onions forming a fourth group. Other groups are fitted in as required. Fig. 14 sums it up.

You can start anywhere on the cycle. Where you had legumes last year, you put brassicas; where you had brassicas last year, you put roots, and so on.

None of this applies unless you are growing vegetables on a relatively large scale; if space is limited, you are unlikely to be growing potatoes. If you are just growing a few vegetables, you can put them in here and there, all mixed up.

There are various standard pest-control techniques. Putting small collars of felt or similar material around the base of brassica plants stops cabbage root-fly from going down the stem to the roots; a barrier about 60 cm (2 ft) high around a bed of carrots will keep out most carrot fly. There are very fine mesh, translucent nets such as 'Papronet' or 'Agryl P' that will keep out all manner of insect pests on many crops. Slugs can be kept out by various barriers, or trapped in ingenious ways, or, along with other large pests, such as caterpillars and sawfly larvae, picked off by hand. Aphids can also be controlled manually — you simply run your fingers and thumb up the affected area, and with broad beans a simple remedy is to pinch out the tops of the plants where the black bean aphid is concentrated.

Grease bands can be put around fruit tree trunks to stop pests crawling up. But fungus diseases cannot be controlled by mechanical means. A favourite technique among 'organic' gardeners to save space and to reduce the need for weeding is to grow vegetables very close together, but this may encourage fungus diseases because the humidity of the air around plants is increased and fungi thrive in humid conditions. Also, insect pests and slugs can hide more easily if plants are grown very close together. The practice of growing one crop adjacent to another, such as carrots and onions, with the idea that the smell or chemical secretions of one plant will ward off the pests of another, known as 'companion planting' is a matter of controversy even within the organic movement.

A good way of preventing fungus diseases is to plant resistant varieties. This applies to a whole range of plants, not just vegetables, and especially roses. However, resistance does not always last for ever, as pests develop strains that overcome the plant's resistance. Varieties of plants may also be resistant to insect attack — the earliest and most famous example of this was when Phylloxera nearly wiped out the European wine industry 100 years ago. It was found that American vine species, although no use for wine, were resistant to the insect, which feeds mainly on roots, so European vine cultivars were grafted onto American rootstocks. Phylloxera, though not eliminated, is no longer a serious grapevine pest.

Biological controls are much talked about as the thing to come, but at present there are few successful techniques that are practicable. There are so few, I can name them all: cabbage caterpillars can be sprayed with a bacterium, Bacillus thuringiensis, which kills them. This is actually sold as a pesticide — e.g. Bactospeine — since it can be applied in the same way and is often mixed with pyrethrum for luck.

Trichoderma is a fungus which can be introduced to fruit trees as a protection against silver-leaf disease, which is also a fungus. In glasshouses, red spider mite and glasshouse whitefly are pests that are resistant to most chemicals but can be controlled by predators. Phytoseiulis persimilis is a mite which eats red spider mite, and Encarsia formosa is a parasite wasp which controls whitefly. This can be a tricky business since there must always be enough of the pest remaining for the predator to survive, and the temperature in the glasshouse is also important.

Pheromones in general are chemicals produced by insects to convey various messages to each other: ants produce trail-marking pheromones, and alarm pheromones cause aphids to drop off the plant. Sex pheromones are produced to attract the opposite sex, and this can be manipulated to control insect pests: a female pheromone will attract male insects to a trap — females in the area will remain unfertilized and so will not breed. This has been used to control tsetse fly in Africa. For the gardener, a pheromone trap is available from HDRA for luring male codling moths whose larvae are the maggots you find in apples and pears. In America attempts have been made to breed predators, such as ladybirds and lacewings, on a large scale, for sale and release by farmers and growers, but no one is trying this in Britain at the moment. It is neither cheap nor easy, and timing is crucial.

However, biological control on an informal basis is the cornerstone or organic philosophy: a rich diversity of many forms of life creates a better ecosystem where no one element takes over. This is much easier in a decorative rather than a productive garden, particularly if we grow plants well suited to their situation. There are many more serious pests and diseases of food crops than of shrubs and herbaceous perennials, and unless we insist on growing plants like hostas, even slugs and snails are not too much of a problem once plants are established. Even lawns are relatively easy if the ground is well prepared, well drained, the appropriate grasses used and a few weeds tolerated. Moss killers will kill moss, but they will not make grass grow if conditions are wrong.

There are decorative plants that can be grown to attract pest predators; the poached egg plant (Limnanthes douglasii), calendula (pot marigold) and nemophila (baby blue-eyes) will attract flies, and umbellifers, such as fennel and dill, attract tiny ichneumon wasps that also feed on aphids.

On a commercial scale, combining minimal pesticide use with biological and cultivation control is known as Integral Pest Management or IPM. It is a great idea, but so far it has not quite taken off in practice. It involves very detailed knowledge of pest and predator life cycles, and very precise knowledge of the side effects of pesticides. For example, a fungicide used to treat a disease might have a significant effect on an insect pest predator as well so the two factors have to be considered and a calculation (or guess) made about which is likely to be more harmful, the fungus or the fungicide. A full IPM scheme also involves weeds with decisions on which weeds are to be eliminated, and which are to be spared because they are food plants for pest predators. The gardener who does everything possible to control pests by other means, but who uses pesticides in desperate situations, is operating a sort of informal IPM scheme.

There is, of course, less profit for agrochemical multinationals in the decreased use of pesticides, and the future is likely to be dominated by what is known as biotechnology, which can mean many things. Genetic engineering could produce improved strains of Rhizobium, the nitrogen-fixing bacterium that lives on legume roots, or even species of Rhizobium that would live in the roots of other plant families. We could imagine a sci-fi nightmare scenario where maverick nitrogen-fixing bacteria invade all plant roots, deplete the atmosphere of nitrogen and swamp the earth with luxuriant growth. But seriously, if these could be developed they could be patented and sold instead of nitrogen fertilizer. Similarly, strains of any plant resistant to any insect or fungus, with improved flavour, extending cropping or uniform size could be created by genetic engineering. Agrochemical multinationals are buying up seed firms fast, possibly with this in mind. They are even developing plant cultivars that are resistant to their own herbicides, so that farmers can carry on using herbicides, even less carefully, without harming the crop being grown. Profits can be maximized by selling both seed and pesticide.

The other area of biotechnology that is already with us and growing fast is micropropagation. This involves chopping up virus-free meristem tissue (growing tips) of selected plant varieties into tiny pieces and growing them in a sterile culture made of agar, sugar, mineral salts, vitamins, and growth hormones. One cutting can produce hundreds of plants, and in no time commercially useful numbers of a new plant variety are ready for sale. All manner of plants from strawberries to begonias are produced in this manner — and they are genetically identical. The potential for good and the potential for harm are probably equal, as with other technologies. One danger is the reduction of the 'gene pool' with just a few 'super' varieties of every plant dominating the market, at risk of being wiped out by some unexpected disease.

How the organic movement will come to terms with this kind of development is an interesting question. The power of the new technologies rather eclipses some of the worries of the 'organic' gardener. If the 'organic' gardener says he will accept genetically engineered seeds and plants cloned on tissue culture as long as no artificial pesticides, hormones or fertilizers have been used to produce them, he might just as well say he will accept nuclear power stations as long as coal-fired central heating is used in the staff canteen!

It would be more consistent to doggedly refuse to have anything to do with it, and stick only to 'natural' things. Alternatively, the organic movement might be able to get actively involved in this new technology and try to encourage the useful and positive aspects of it (such as disease resistance and flavour), but this would mean a redefinition of itself. Specifically, it would mean accepting that the 'artificial' or 'natural' origin of a chemical does not define its harmful or beneficial qualities, and pales into insignificance when faced with the power of the new technologies that are upon us.

A garden can be almost anything: it can be a reflection of ourselves or our aspirations, it can be a Zen garden full of stones, it can be a farm in miniature, it can be an escape from reality, or a burden to be escaped from. Voltaire's Candide, after innumerable trials and terrible hardships, settles down to work on his little farm which is all he has left in the world. From then on, every time his doggedly optimistic companion philosophizes about 'This best of all possible worlds,' his reply is *Il faut cultiver son jardin*.

The world has changed and shrunk since Voltaire's time and owning a small farm is the dream of many and the privilege of a few rather than the last resort of the exhausted. We can still 'cultivate our gardens', however small, but we cannot pretend that the rest of the world does not exist. Just over the wall a new office block or a bypass is being built, hedgerows are being grubbed up, and woodland felled. On television we can witness environmental destruction on a grander scale, and we as individuals are part of the process as we drive back from the supermarket with our plastic bags full of packaged goods and, maybe, even some film-wrapped 'organic' vegetables on a plastic tray.

# A to Z

The following list includes chemical elements, compounds, types of fertilizer, types of pesticide, and a variety of substances, and related terms. Many are mentioned in the main text, and the reader is referred to the relevant chapter; others are given a lengthier description if of interest and not mentioned elsewhere. Individual pesticides are found in the tables following this section, along with brands of pesticide and 'organic' products.

*Acaricide* Many insecticides also kill mites and other small animals. Some mites, such as glasshouse red spider mite, are very serious pests; others are predators.

*Acid/Alkali* Rainwater, water in soil, in fertilizer solutions, etc., all contain substances which make them slightly acid or alkaline (basic). This is measured on the pH scale, which goes from 1 to 14, where 7 is neutral. The range normally encountered in natural environment is from 4 to 8.5. Different plant nutrients become more or less soluble and therefore available under different levels of acidity or basicity, and consequently different plants, soil micro-organisms and soil animals thrive accordingly. Slightly acid, about pH 6.5, is regarded as ideal as most

plants will do well at that level. Deviation by much either side is only tolerated by specialized plants.

*Aerosol* A fine spray expelled from a canister by gas under pressure (propellant). The most popular propellant until recently was chlorofluorocarbon (CFC) which was considered ideal — non-flammable, non-toxic — until its effect on the ozone layer and as a 'greenhouse' gas was discovered. Many household fly sprays come in an aerosol can — for other purposes it is not economic.

*Alkali* See Acid/Alkali.

*Aluminium* The third most abundant element in the earth's crust is aluminium, but it is of no direct use to plants or animals. Alumina (aluminium hydroxide) along with silica (see Silicon) are the major components of most clays (see Chapter 4). In this form aluminium is quite inert and, despite the huge quantities all around us, is quite harmless. However, when released from this form into solution it behaves quite differently and has recently been the subject of much concern — it may be related to Alzheimer's Disease (early senile dementia). Cooking fruit in aluminium pans might be avoided for this reason.

Acid soils, especially on certain rock types, tend to release a lot of aluminium into the water supply, which, owing to the chemical properties of the aluminium ion, further increases acidity, and so on: this is known as acidification, and is aggravated by acid rain from industry.

*Aluminium sulphate* This has the ability to attract small particles, and is therefore used to clarify water. The scandal over contaminated water in Camelford, Cornwall, in 1988, was caused by large amounts of aluminium sulphate being dumped into the wrong container. It is also used as a blueing compound for hydrangeas because it has powerful properties to neutralize alkalinity — hydrangeas are only blue in an acid environment. It is also the main ingredient in 'organic' slug killers and, in many people's experience, rather ineffective. It should not be used in quantity, especially if your soil is acid to start with.

*Ammonium* This is $NH_4^+$, a base, a cation. In fertilizers, such as ammonium nitrate and ammonium sulphate, it is a major supplier of nitrogen. As a cation it can be adsorbed to the clay-humus complex in the soil, and is therefore not leached out as nitrate ($NO_3^-$, anion) is. However, as plants generally take up their nitrogen as nitrate it must be converted by soil micro-organisms to nitrate first.

*Ammonium nitrate* $NH_4NO_3$ is second only to urea in its proportion of nitrogen (35 per cent).

*Ammonium sulphate* This contains 10 per cent nitrogen.

*Anion* A negatively charged ion.

*Anticholinesterase* This nerve poison works by inhibiting the enzyme cholinesterase. Organophosphate and carbamate pesticides work on this principle.

*Arsenic (As)* A rare element (.00005 per cent of earth's crust), a metal, and general biocide, but traces are apparently necessary to health of animals. Lead arsenate and sodium arsenite were both used in the past as herbicides but are rarely used now because of their general toxicity to most life forms. Denis Thatcher's fortune has its origins in sodium arsenite: his grandfather founded Atlas Preservatives to market sodium arsenite as a sheep dip. It did less harm to the sheep than to the sheep's parasites and was widely used until something better turned up.

*Auxin* This was the first of the natural plant-growth hormones to be identified, and is also known as beta-indolyl acetic acid or IAA. Chemically related synthetic substances are used as hormone rooting powders, or as weedkillers (see Hormone).

*Bark* Finely shredded bark, composted to kill off any harmful fungi, etc., is used as a mulch for trees and shrubs and on paths.

*Base* Base equals alkali (see Acid).

*Basic slag* A by-product of the steel industry, basic slag contains useful amounts of phosphate (8-18 per cent), lime, and sulphur. Regarded as a slow-release phosphate fertilizer, it is approved by organic standards.

*Bicarbonate of soda* See Sodium.

*Biocide* A complete poison, which works on most or all forms of life.

*Blood* Dried blood is a high nitrogen fertilizer — about 10 per cent — usually mixed with fish and bone meal to make a more balanced supply of nutrients. Although completely 'natural' and 'organic', its use is frowned upon by purists because of its high solubility, and therefore immediate availability to plants, which makes it resemble a chemical fertilizer. A good compost heap activator, it is more expensive than a 'chemical' nitrogen product.

*Bonemeal* A slow-release phosphate fertilizer, bonemeal contains some nitrogen as well, and is acceptable by organic standards.

*Boron (B)* Although an essential trace element for plants, boron is not required by animals. The tiny amount plants require is usually available in soil. Borax (sodium tetraborate) can be applied to soil if it is certain there is a deficiency, but in larger quantities it is used as an insecticide (for ants) and even as a total, and very persistent, weedkiller.

*Broad-spectrum* These pesticides affect a wide variety of pests as opposed to working *selectively* or *specifically*.

*Buckwheat* See Green manures.

*Cadmium (Cd)* See Heavy metals.

*Calcium (Ca)* An essential element for animals and plants, required in fairly large amounts, calcium is known as a macronutrient. It is normally very abundant in soil and therefore not regarded as a 'fertilizer'. The abundance of the calcium ion in soil is the major factor in determining its alkalinity or acidity. Calcium is applied to soil either in compound fertilizers, such as calcium nitrate (nitrochalk), or as ground chalk or limestones (calcium carbonate). Lime, as it is also known, should not be applied at the same time as manure or ammonium fertilizer, since they react and the ammonium breaks down giving off ammonia gas, and so wasting the nitrogen in the fertilizer.

*Carbamate* Carbamate is a type of chemical which includes insecticides and herbicides. See Anticholinesterase.

*Carbon (C)* Carbon is the core of every molecule in living matter. Carbon atoms — built up in rings and chains with atoms or other elements, especially hydrogen and oxygen, hooked on around them — are what we

and all life forms are made of (see Chapter 1). The 'carbon cycle' involves photosynthesis and respiration (see Chapter 4) where carbon dioxide passes from the atmosphere into plants, then into animals, and is returned to the atmosphere when animals breathe out or when plant residues decompose. For a breathtaking ride around the carbon cycle, read the last chapter of Primo Levi's *The Periodic Table*, which is not a chemical treatise, but a collection of mostly autobiographical stories by a chemist. Very little carbon dioxide is actually present in the atmosphere, most of it being dissolved in the oceans or incorporated in living matter and fossil fuels which were once living matter. The proportion of carbon dioxide in the atmosphere is only about 0.03 per cent of the total, although burning fossil fuels has measurably increased this proportion recently, giving rise to fears of a 'greenhouse effect'. This is because carbon dioxide (and some other gases) will allow light from the sun through to the earth, but the lower frequencies of light are reflected back and absorbed by these gases. This is comparable with what happens when light travels through glass, and why greenhouses warm up.

*Carcinogen* A carcinogen is anything that causes cancer. Many pesticides are either positive or suspected carcinogens, but it should be remembered that many natural substances, and some things essential to life itself — sunlight, for example — are also carcinogens (see Chapter 5).

*Catalyst* See Synergist.

*Cation* This is a postively charged ion, e.g., $K^+$: see Ion.

*Chalk* A kind of limestone, chalk is very common in south-east England (see Calcium).

*Chelate* A word coming from the Greek *chelos*, meaning claw. Chelation is a kind of chemical bond where a complex organic compound holds on to a mineral ion. In very alkaline soils, where nutrients such as iron, manganese and magnesium may be unavailable to plants, chelated compounds — also called 'sequestrols' — may be applied to the soil or sprayed direct on to leaves. This is expensive, and not a large-scale solution to the problem. Some modern plant foods contain chelated micro-nutrients. Chelates are not suitable for the strict organic gardener. Fortunately, humus is full of natural chelating agents, so this is another reason for ensuring a good organic content in the soil.

*Chlorine*  This is poisonous green gas, but not found in this form in nature! The chlorine atoms hooked on to many organic pesticide molecules — as in *chlor*dane, hexa*chloro*hexane, etc — are often the parts that make them poisonous, but many other substances containing chlorine (such as common salt, sodium chloride) are not poisonous. Both sodium and chloride ions are found in plants in much greater quantities than required. Sodium in fact, is not regarded as necessary at all for plants, but chloride is essential in tiny quantities for photosynthesis.

*Chlorophyll*  The green, and also yellow and orange, substances in leaves that absorb light energy to power the process of photosynthesis. The leaf colour that we see is the part of the spectrum that is reflected: the parts of the spectrum that are absorbed are blue and red.

*Clay*  See Chapter 4.

*Clover*  See Green manures.

*Colloid*  Clay and humus are both colloids — meaning 'glue-like'. Usually in soil they are bound up together as the 'clay-humus complex', and being negatively charged can adsorb plant nutrient cations such as ammonium, potassium and magnesium (see Chapter 4).

*Comfrey*  This is one of the 'trademarks' of organic gardening. The Henry Doubleday Research Association (HDRA), Britain's largest organic gardening organization, is named after Henry Doubleday who investigated the many qualities of the plant. As a herbal medicine, Comfrey is reputed to relieve stomach problems and accelerate the healing of wounds and arthritis, but it is also grown as a perennial green manure. 'Bocking 14', the variety available from HDRA, can be cut several times a year and used either as high-potash mulch or liquid feed. It is also a 'suspected carcinogen'.

*Compost*  See Chapter 6.

*Compound*  A compound is any substance that is not a pure element. Copper (Cu) is an element. Copper sulphate ($CuSO_4$) is a compound.

*Compound fertilizer*  This is a fertilizer that supplies more than one major plant food either as a single chemical, such as potassium nitrate, supplying both potassium (K) and nitrogen (N), or as a mixture of chemicals such as a 'balanced' fertilizer like Growmore.

*Copper (Cu)*  An essential trace element for plants, copper is found in various enzymes, and is also important in photosynthesis. In large quantities it is a general biocide, and is a useful fungicide, approved by organic standards (see Chapter 5).

*Cow manure*  See Chapter 6 and Farmyard manure.

*Dioxin*  Dioxin or TCDD is one of the deadliest poisons. Traces are produced in various chemical manufacturing processes, from bleaching to the manufacture of the herbicide 2, 4, 5-T.

*Dirty Dozen*  A campaign was launched in 1985 to ban the use of 12 of the most dangerous pesticides. Of the 12, three are still registered for amateur use: gamma HCH (lindane), paraquat and 2, 4, 5-T. The last, though still registered, is no longer formulated for amateur use.

*Dithiocarbamates* These are a group of non-systemic fungicides including thiram and mancozeb. Developed long before the recent worries about pesticides, they have now been re-investigated and are regarded as potential carcinogens.

*Dolomite* The Dolomites are a range of mountains along the Austrian and Italian border, composed of a mixture of calcium carbonate (limestone) and magnesium carbonate. Dolomite is a useful source of magnesium for slow release, and is favoured by organic gardeners, but as it also acts like ordinary lime to raise the soil pH, it is not suitable for very alkaline soils.

*Dried blood* See Blood.

*Dust* Some pesticides are formulated as dust to be applied dry (as opposed to a 'wettable powder'). Since they are not to be diluted, the proportion of active ingredient is low — maybe 1-5 per cent. Although useful in situations where water is scarce, dusts are not good otherwise because they do not cling to leaf surfaces — especially not the underside where many pests are found.

*Elder* Half a kilo of elderleaves simmered for half an hour in four litres of water, then strained, may work as an 'organic' fungicide. It is also suggested for killing aphids.

*Element* Oxygen is an element; it exists in the atmosphere as molecules composed of two atoms.

*Encarsia formosa* This is a parasitic wasp, predator of glasshouse whitefly. (See Chapter 7).

*Epsom salts* This is magnesium sulphate, a useful source of magnesium. The sulphate gives it an acid reaction, as it is better than

dolomite on alkaline soils. Being easily soluble, it does not last long in soil, and is frowned upon by organic standards.

*Farmyard manure* Generally a mixture of cow dung and straw, farmyard manure is a 'cold' manure, meaning that it decays anaerobically, without giving off heat. It contains, on average, about 0.5 per cent nitrogen (N) 0.25 per cent phosphorus (P) and 0.35 per cent potassium (K).

*Feldspar* Feldspar is a type of rock, some forms of which contain useful amounts of potassium, which can be used as a very slow release potassium fertilizer.

*Fenugreek* See Green manures.

*Fishmeal* Containing about 10 per cent nitrogen, and about 15 per cent phosphate, fishmeal is usually sold with blood and bonemeal.

*Flowers of sulphur* See Sulphur.

*Foliar spray* Plants normally take in nutrients through their roots, but just as they can absorb pesticides through their leaves, they can absorb nutrients too. Foliar sprays promote the growth of leaves over the rest of the plant, and should be discontinued when plants reach the flowering stage, after which liquid feeding can continue to the soil. Sequestrols (chelates) can also be sprayed on for instant correction of micro-nutrient deficiences.

*Formulation* This is the form in which pesticides are available: emulsion, granules, dust, etc. (See Chapter 5).

*Fumigant* A fumigant is a specialized formulation of insecticide for use in greenhouses where the active ingredient is incorporated into flammable mixture to produce a dense smoke.

*General-purpose compost* This is for sowing seeds and cuttings as well as for established plants (see Chapter 6).

*Grazing rye*  See Green manures.

*Grease band*  This provides a non-toxic way of protecting fruit trees. Insects — various moth caterpillars — crawling up the trunk encounter the barrier and go no further. It is used from autumn to spring.

*Green manures*  If you grow vegetables, there is always bare earth when a crop has been cleared. This may be spring or autumn. Rather than leave the soil bare to get re-infested with weeds, or to have the nutrients washed out by rain, especially in winter, a crop such as mustard or grazing rye can be sown, which is either dug in when the ground is needed again, or composted. Some green manures such as clover, being legumes, can fix nitrogen from the air (see Chapter 4). Some, such as grazing rye, are hardy and can be over-wintered, or, like alfalfa and comfrey, grown for years and cut regularly for compost material. Others, like buckwheat or mustard, are very quick growing and only occupy the ground for a couple of months. Leguminous green manures include red clover, fenugreek, lupin, trefoil, winter field beans and winter tares. It is not a practical consideration for a small garden.

*Ground Rock Phosphate (GRP)*  See Rock phosphate.

*Growmore*  Growmore is a balanced 7-7-7 NPK fertilizer, developed during the Second World War for the Dig-For-Britain campaign. It tends to be used indiscriminately by some gardeners on vegetables, flowers and shrubs alike, as an addition to, or sometimes instead of, compost and manure.

*Growth regulator*  Hormones are growth regulators; synthetic hormones are used as weedkillers, as rooting powders for assisting in the establishment of cuttings, and as a means of suppressing the growth of hedges so that they do not need clipping. They are also used commercially to stop stored potatoes from sprouting. All growth regulators are unacceptable by organic standards.

*Gypsum*  This is calcium sulphate. Adding lime (calcium carbonate) to clay soil improves its texture, causing the clay to 'flocculate' or break up into cultivable crumbs. Some clays are very alkaline, so using gypsum, the alkalinity of which is relieved by the sulphate, enables this to be done without increasing alkalinity. It is approved by organic standards.

*Heavy metals*  Various metals are sometimes found in high concentration in soil, especially in towns. Some of these — copper, zinc, manganese — are essential trace elements when present in minute quantities, but poisons in larger concentrations. But cadmium and lead are of no use to plants or animals and are regarded as undesirable in any concentration. Lead is, of course, most concentrated in towns because of the lead content in petrol. Concern about the levels of metals in home-grown vegetables has been allayed recently, since it was found that plants filter out unwanted metals very effectively, and even where metals are in high concentration in the soil, plants do not take them up very much. In one experiment in 1986, where lead in gardens in Central London was at 400 parts per million, most plants still contained much less than one part per million.

*Home-made sprays*  Nettles, rhubarb, elder, garlic, cigarette butts and many other things can be prepared at home for pest control, but under the 1986 regulations it is illegal to use anything but registered products as pesticides.

*Hoof and horn*  A slow-release source of nitrogen, hoof and horn is frequently a component of balanced organic fertilizers.

*Hops*  'Spent' hops are a by-product of brewing beer, and can be used as a soil conditioner — if you can get them, which is unlikely.

*Hormone*   See Growth regulator.

*Horse manure*   This is one of the best animal manures, but often made with wood-shavings rather than straw. This can be a problem because woodshavings are much slower to rot and can cause a nitrogen deficiency if dug in too soon. Known as 'hot' manure because it gives off heat as it decomposes, horse manure used to be buried in trenches to create a 'hot bed' to give heat to early crops in the days before heated greenhouses.

*Humus*   See Chapters 4 and 6.

*Hydrogen*   This is the smallest and lightest of all elements and, in the form of water and carbohydrates, one of the most important components of living organisms. Acidity, the pH of the soil, is a measure of the amount of hydrogen ions ($H^+$) present.

*Insecticidal soaps*   See Soap.

*Ion*   Ions have nothing at all to do with *iron*. Inorganic compounds that are soluble in water are composed of ions: cations are positively charged and are balanced by negatively charged anions. Some ions have more than one charge, so the 'formula' of a compound may be complicated in order that the whole thing should be electrically balanced — aluminium sulphate $Al^{+++}_2 (SO_4^{--})_3$, for example (see Chapter 1).

*Iron*   An essential element for plants and animals, iron is required in small amounts for photosynthesis and respiration. A deficiency shows up as 'chlorosis', a yellowing of the leaves.

*Irritant*   Many substances that are not serious poisons are nevertheless irritants to the eyes or skin, or when inhaled.

*John Innes Compost*   See Chapter 6.

*K*   This is the chemical symbol for potassium, from the Latin *Kalium*.

*Kainite*   A source of potassium as potassium chloride combined with magnesium sulphate, Kainite may contain large amounts of common salt as well, which makes it unreliable.

*Kelp*   A kind of seaweed, kelp (ascophyllum nodosum) is the most common type used for liquid seaweed fertilizer products.

*Lawn sand*   A mixture of sand, ferrous sulphate and ammonium sulphate, lawn sand kills moss and broad-leaved weeds, but fertilizes the grass in a lawn.

*Lead*   See Heavy metals.

*Leafmould*   See Chapter 6.

*Legumes*   The pea and bean family, legumes are unique and important because their roots grow symbiotically with Rhizobium bacteria which fix nitrogen from the air (see Chapter 4).

*Light*   No one knows precisely what light is, whether it is waves or particles, but what is known is that it is the energy source that keeps the world alive. Different wavelengths have different uses. Part of the ultraviolet spectrum — very high frequency — is destructive and carcinogenic, but it is also essential for vitamin D synthesis. Blue and red are the wavelengths required for photosynthesis, while infra-red, very low frequency, is the part that feels warm.

*Lime*   See Calcium.

*Liquid manure/feed*   This is any solution source of plant nutrients, whether of natural or artificial origin, heavily diluted and watered on so as to be immediately available to plant roots (see also foliar sprays).

*Loam*   Has two distinct meanings. First, a soil comprising ideal proportions of sand, silt and clay. Second, rotted turves used as an ingredient in John Innes type composts.

*Lupin*  See Green manures.

*Macronutrients*  These are substances of which plants need relatively large amounts. The main ones are nitrogen, phosphate and potassium, followed by calcium, magnesium and sulphur and iron. The micronutrients, or trace elements — manganese, zinc, copper, boron, molybdenum and chlorine — are required in much smaller amounts.

*Magnesium (Mg)*  A macronutrient, magnesium forms part of the chlorophyll molecule. Deficiency shows as chlorosis with leaves becoming yellow between the veins.

*Manganese (Mn)*  A trace element, manganese activates certain enzymes.

*Mercury (Hg)*  Mercury salts, and particularly organic compounds, are highly toxic. Mercurous chloride, or calomel, is still available to amateurs as a fungicide for treating clubroot in brassicas and onion white rot.

*Micronutrients*  See Macronutrients.

*Mineral*  This has two distinct meanings. First, different types of rock; e.g. quartz, calcite, feldspar. Second, various nutrients in the form that plants can use them, i.e. simple inorganic ions, such as phosphate, nitrate, potassium.

*Molluscicide*  This kills slugs and snails.

*Molybdenum (Mb)*  A trace element, molybdenum is required for nitrogen fixation in plants.

*Mulch*  A layer of material over the soil to conserve moisture, suppress weeds, and conserve heat in winter. Mulches can be made from almost anything: compost, manure, peat, bark, leaf mould, newspaper, or plastic sheeting.

*Muriate*  'Muriate of potash' is potassium chloride, the most common and cheapest potassium fertilizer. If you are going to use a 'chemical' fertilizer, potassium sulphate is generally better. Chloride ions are not much use to plants or soil; sulphate is needed in greater quantity, and some crops actually suffer: potatoes tend to be more watery and with a rather soapy flavour.

*Mushroom compost*  Mushrooms are grown in various mixtures of peat, farmyard or horse manure, soil and lime. When a few crops have been grown, it is discarded and sold off as 'spent mushroom compost'.

*Mustard*  See Green manures.

*Mutagens*  These cause genetic damage (see Chapter 5).

*Nematicide*  Nematodes are also known as eelworms. Some are large enough to see with the naked eye, but it is the microscopic ones that are the serious plant pests, different species being pests of potato, onion, tomato, phlox, strawberry etc. They can remain in the soil as 'cysts' for many years waiting to strike again when their host plant is grown again. Soil sterilants can control them in the greenhouse, but on a large scale they can not be eliminated, except by not growing the affected crop for several years. Crop rotation helps prevent eelworm infestation in the first place. See also Tagetes minuta.

*Nettles*  Very resilient weeds, nettles nevertheless have their uses. They are the larval food plant of several attractive butterflies, can be made into soup, liquid manure and possibly to kill aphids — though it is more likely that the addition of soap as a wetting agent is actually the active ingredient.

*Nicotine*  A powerful insecticide, nicotine is no longer available to amateurs.

*Nitrogen (N)*  Nitrogen is one of the three main macronutrients of plants. The 'Nitrogen cycle' involves the transformation of gas in the atmosphere to part of living organisms, its transfer between micro-organisms, plants and animals, and its ultimate re-release into the atmosphere.

*Nitrate* ($NO_3^-$) These anions are the main form in which plants take up nitrogen. Typical nitrate fertilizers are ammonium nitrate (34 per cent N) and calcium nitrate (17 per cent N).

*Organochlorine* These insecticides — DDT and lindane, for example — were the first pesticides used on a large scale (see Chapters 2 and 5).

*Organomercury* These fungicides, such as phenyl mercury acetate, are used for seed dressing and are among the most toxic chemicals used. Not available to amateurs.

*Organophosphates* These are the most heavily used insecticides at the moment (see Chapters 2 and 5).

*Peat* See Chapter 6.

*Persistent pesticides* These last a long time in soil or plant before decomposing. It is impossible to say exactly how persistent a pesticide is: it will vary according to the formulation, whether it is in the soil, in the plant as a systemic, or on the leaf; according to the weather, and the acidity of the soil. A standard way of measuring persistence is by its 'half-life' — the time it takes for half of it to decompose. Pyrethrum, and some of the synthetic pyrethroids, are 'non-persistent', and break down rapidly in light and air. 'Short persistence' involves a few days, 'medium persistence' a few weeks, and 'long persistence' months or even years, as in the case of DDT.

*Pheromone Traps* See Chapter 7.

*Phosphorus (P)* A major plant nutrient, phosphorus is taken in by plants as phosphate ion $H_2PO_4^-$. Phosphate fertilizers include ammonium phosphate (24 per cent P) and triple super phosphate (20 per cent P).

*Phytoseiulis persimilis* This is a mite which is a predator of the greenhouse red spider mite. See Chapter 7.

*Phytotoxin* 'Phyto-' is the scientist's prefix for anything to do with plants, so a phytotoxin is something poisonous to plants. Many pesticides are phytotoxic to a degree, either to particular species or plants, if the weather is hot or dry, or if used under-diluted.

*Pigeon manure* Unless you live near a pigeon fancier, this manure is unlikely to be on offer. Very rich in nitrogen, it would make a good compost heap activator.

*Pig manure* Like farmyard manure, pig manure is a cold manure, rotting slowly without heat. It contains about 0.5 per cent N, 0.5 per cent P, 0.35 per cent K.

*Post-emergent herbicides* See Chapter 5.

*Potassium (K)* or *potash* The third of the major plant nutrients. Potassium fertilizers include 'muriate of potash' — potassium chloride (50 per cent K), potassium sulphate (44 per cent K), postassium nitrate (36 per cent K).

*Potassium permanganate* Permanganate of potash is a straightforward, highly corrosive poison in its concentrated form. In various dilutions it has been used as an insecticide, fungicide, moss killer and slug killer. It is one of the few chemicals permitted by organic standards as a soil sterilant.

*Potting compost* See Chapter 6.

*Poultry manure* High in nitrogen, poultry manure is a good compost-heap activator, and contains about 2.5 per cent nitrogen, 2 per cent phosphorus and 1 per cent potassium.

*Pre-emergent herbicide* See Chapter 5.

*Pyrethroid* These are the group of artificial insecticides chemically related to natural pyrethrum (see Chapter 5).

*Quassia* A tropical bark product with some insecticidal qualities, quassia has very low toxicity. It is also sold as a dog and cat repellant.

*Residual pesticides* These do not break down quickly — particularly soil-acting herbicides (see Chapter 5).

*Rhizobium* This is the famous bacterium that lives in the root hairs of plants of the legume family and refixes atmospheric nitrogen. It is not normally missing from soils in temperate climates, but can be encouraged if necessary — if soil is very acid — by coating seeds in a mixture containing it before sowing.

*Rhubarb* Leaves of rhubarb can be made into a spray with a reputed insecticidal effect.

*Rock phosphate* Rock phosphate is the raw material from which commercial phosphate fertilizers are derived. Applied in its original form, it is very slowly released. Along with bonemeal, it is the strict organic gardener's only phosphate fertilizer (see Chapter 4).

*Rock potash* This is an extremely slow-release source of potassium, and has little immediate effect on plant growth (see Chapter 4).

*Rodenticides* These kill rats, mice, moles, and maybe your pets.

*Rooting powder* A hormone rooting powder contains various substances similar to natural hormones, which stimulate rooting of cuttings when used in the right concentrations. The same substances in different concentrations will retard growth, kill plants, or stimulate fruit production.

*Rye* See Green manures.

*Salt* Common salt is sodium chloride; other salts are plant nutrients (see Chapters 1 and 4).

*Sand* Sand is one of the main ingredients of soil. Sand is defined as particles between 0.02 mm and 2 mm across. It is made of inert pieces of silicate, and is also an ingredient of soil-less potting composts (see Chapter 4).

*Sawdust* Sawdust is definitely something to be avoided in the garden. It takes ages to rot down and if dug into soil will deplete its nitrogen.

*Seaweed* It contains about 0.5 per cent nitrogen, 0.2 per cent phosphorus and 2 per cent potassium and is most commonly available as a liquid feed, but can also be composted or dug in direct to the ground where it improves the soil texture. Kelp is considered the best. There is also 'calcified seaweed', a coral-like seaweed containing large amounts of calcium and magnesium, which is also useful as an alternative to lime for increasing soil pH. Seaweed products are said to contain natural plant hormones — cytokinins — and this is what the manufacturers of Maxicrop mean by ' biostimulant'.

*Seed compost* See Chapter 6.

*Seed dressing* Seeds may be coated with fungicide and insecticide to protect them before and during germination, but this is not approved of by organic standards. Many seeds come ready dressed in the packet, although there is no indication on the packet to say so, or with what. Undressed seed is available from various organic suppliers.

*Selective pesticides* As opposed to *total*, or broad spectrum pesticides (see Chapter 5).

*Sequestrol* See Chelate.

*Sewage sludge* Not something you can get from the garden centre, sewage sludge's nutrient content varies with how it has been treated, but generally it contains more nitrogen than phosphorus than or potassium. The main problem with sewage is eliminating all the poisonous industrial and domestic wastes that go into it. At present most sewage is dumped into the sea, untreated. Four thousand million cubic metres of untreated sewage go into the North Sea annually.

*Silicon* This is the second most abundant element on earth. Sand and silt are composed of particles of silicate — silicon oxide; clays are composed of various combinations of silica and alumina (see Chapter 4).

*Silt* Silt consists of soil particles smaller than sand but larger than clay.

*Slow release fertilizer* The less soluble fertilizers are, the more slowly they are released to the plant. However, soluble fertilizers can be incorporated in a less soluble medium, like the 'tabs' that supply pot plants for a whole season (see *Soluble fertilizers*) See CHEMPAK in list of addresses, p. 101.

*Soap* This has been used as an insecticide for at least 100 years, but went out of use with the invention of DDT *et al*. Recently it has come back into favour because of its low toxicity and non-persistence (see Chapter 5).

*Sodium* (Na) A vital element for animals, but not for plants, sodium is nevertheless present in plants. Sodium usually comes in tandem with chloride, as common salt. In any more than traces, salt is a problem in soil, and in larger amounts is an effective total weedkiller.

*Sodium bicarbonate* (Also called sodium hydrogencarbonate and bicarbonate of soda) is well known as a remedy for acid indigestion. It has recently been found to work quite well as a fungicide — especially for mildews.

*Sodium tetraborate* See Boron.

*Soft soap* It is weaker than 'insecticidal' soap and is less likely to damage the plant. See Soap.

*Soil* See Chapter 4.

*Soil conditioner* This is any substance that improves the texture of soil. This is carried out by any bulky organic matter, such as compost, peat or manure, but also by a chemical action known as flocculation. Lime, gypsum, even PVA (wallpaper paste) and particularly seaweed have this effect. A heavy clay soil is broken down into a more crumbly and airy structure, and a light sandy soil is bound up into a more crumbly structure. Humus also acts in this way, so compost and manure when decomposed ultimately do the same thing.

*Soil organisms* A vast range of creatures, from wireworms, centipedes and earthworms to fungi and bacteria occupy soil. There are parasites feeding on other living organisms; saprophytes, feeding on dead matter; nitrifiers, denitrifiers, and so on. Obviously some are directly useful — such as earthworms which aerate soil and, as they feed, process soil and dead organic matter into a form more useful to plants. Centipedes are predators of many soil pests, whereas millipedes and wireworms feed on living plant roots. Some bacteria and fungi make minerals available to plants, and others are plant pathogens. Their importance as a whole is appreciated but not understood. There is a general agreement that a soil rich in living organisms is better than one lacking in them, despite the damage that some of them do. The problem with pesticides is that they may damage the beneficial organisms along with the pathogens and pests.

*Soot* Soot contains ammonia and sulphur and may be used as a fertilizer, but the sulphur content is high enough to have some effect controlling soil pests — wireworms, leatherjackets, etc — and beneficial creatures like worms as well. Its blackness assists in absorbing sunlight to warm the soil in spring, but it may also harm plants if used in quantity.

*Spray* Pesticides are mostly applied as sprays. The spraying equipment used by amateurs is usually crude — some fine spray, a lot of coarse spray, and some dribbles. The dilutions recommended for garden pesticides take this into account. Very large droplets simply run off the target; very small droplets stay in the air and may drift far from the target — either way they cause problems. In recent years, ultra-low-volume (ULV) spraying has come into favour: the pesticide is used in a much more concentrated form so that each leaf gets just a few tiny droplets of concentrated pesticide rather than a drench of weak solution. This saves carrying large quantities of liquid around but the problem with drift is worse — there is more of it, and it is more concentrated. The latest development is controlled-droplet-application (CDA), where a spinning, toothed disc throws off almost uniformly sized droplets; the size can be varied by altering the speed of the disc. This offers genuine hope of reduced pesticide requirements, and less danger of drift. The equipment is, of course, very expensive, and amateur gardeners will have to make do with yesterday's technology.

*Sterilant* The ideal sterilant will kill the harmful organisms in soil while sparing the beneficial ones. This is possible to a degree by steaming: weed seeds and pathogens are generally killed at about 60°C, whereas most of the beneficial bacteria and fungi will survive higher temperatures. However, unless you have special steam sterilizing equipment, this is not really practical. The other way is with various chemicals, most of which are not available to the amateur — cresylic acid being an exception. Chemical sterilants are general biocides, which are not used by organic gardeners (except potassium permangamate), and only ever in small areas, such as in glasshouses where rotation of crops is not practicable and pests (for instance tomato eelworm) may build up.

*Sticker* This is a kind of surfactant (surface actant) that actually sticks the pesticide to the leaf. Nu-Film-P is derived from pine resin and is approved by organic standards. Used in tests to establish the efficacy of sodium bicarbonate as a fungicide, it was found to be very effective on its own!

*Stomach poison* See Chapter 5.

*Subsoil* This is the layer between the topsoil and the parent rock. See Chapter 4. When digging, it may be broken up with a fork, but should never be brought to the surface since it is lacking in nutrients and organic matter.

*Sulphur* A major plant nutrient, sulphur is not usually lacking in soil, and never near the sea or downwind from industrial pollution. It is taken up by plants and sulphate ions ($SO_4^{--}$). Amino acids containing sulphur are present in most protein.

Sulphur is one of many substances that are both 'good' and 'bad'. The sulphur dioxide produced by burning coal and oil causes acid rain; but the phytoplankton Emiliana huxleyii with its important role of removing carbon dioxide from the atmosphere, also releases comparable amounts of sulphur, as dimethyl sulphide, to the atmosphere. Elemental sulphur is somewhat poisonous — more so than many synthetic fungicides — and can also damage some sensitive species of plants, may kill mites and insects and is fairly persistent. It is nevertheless, one of the few fungicides approved by organic standards. Also used as smoke for deterring moles.

*Sunshine* See Light.

*Superphosphate* See Phosphorus.

*Surfactant* This means 'surface actant', and is the same as 'wetting agent'. Everyone knows how difficult it is to wet a shiny surface, a fine powder, or a pot of dry peat compost: the water bounces off or goes into globules. Peat-based composts contain a wetting agent to enable them to absorb water easily, and most pesticides contain a wetting agent to enable them to cling to leaves. Surfactants increase the efficiency of pesticides, so that less of the active ingredient has to be used. In some cases they act as pesticides in their own right. Soap is the oldest surfactant, and a useful insecticide. See also Sticker.

*Synergist* This is another word for 'catalyst': a substance that improves the performance of something else without having any direct effect itself. Pesticides that have suffered from the problem of resistance can be given a further lease of life by the addition of a synergist. Some of the safer — less effective — insecticides can also be boosted in this way without apparently increasing the toxicity to mammals. Natural pyrethrum and other synthetic pyrethroids often have piperonyl butoxide added as a synergist.

*Systemic* These pesticides enter the sap stream of a plant (see Chapter 5).

*Tagetes minuta* A relative of the French marigold, its roots secrete chemicals called thiophenes (*thio* is Greek for sulphur) which can have some effect against eelworms and some harmful fungi. It also has some effect against perennial weeds, such as couch grass and ground elder. A kind of living herbicide and soil-sterilant, it grows about 2 metres tall — not a plant for ordinary garden use, but a good source of green manure.

*Tar oil* This is used as a winter wash on fruit trees to kill any pests hibernating in the bark. It also kills 'Anthocoris nemorum', a bug which is a useful predator of fruit tree spider mite. This pest used to feed on the lichens and algae growing on the trunk, but these are also killed by tar oil, so it has now altered its habits and eats leaves instead, with no Anthocoris nemorum to control it. It is an early example of a pest actually created

by pesticides. Heavy use of sulphur is reported to have had a similar effect.

*Tea leaves* Well-diluted tea makes a good high potash feed. Tea leaves also contain a lot of nitrogen which is locked up in tannins and slowly released.

*Teratogen* This is a substance that can cause birth defects after conception, as opposed to a mutagen which alters the genes and does the damage before conception. Thalidomide is the famous, and extreme, example of a teratogen.

*Tin* A moderately poisonous metal, tin is not required by plants or animals. Many wood preservatives contain tri-butyl tin, which was responsible for sex changes in the common dog-whelk as a result of its use as an anti-fouling paint on boats.

*Top-dressing* This is putting fertilizer on the soil surface, rather than digging it in — usually while plants are in active growth. A top dressing of compost or manure is known as a mulch.

*Toxin* Poison.

*Trace element* See Micronutrient.

*Translocated herbicide* The same as *systemic*.

*Triazine* This is a group of herbicides including atrazine and simazine.

*Trichoderma* This is a fungus that can be introduced into fruit trees to protect them from silver-leaf disease, another fungus. It is comparable to the human practice of eating live yoghurt to compete with undesirable organisms like Candida albicans.

*Triplesuperphosphate* See Phosphorus.

*Urea* It is the most concentrated, and most widely used, nitrogen fertilizer, containing 45 per cent nitrogen. Although a manufactured 'chemical' fertilizer, urea is also a natural, organic substance — $(NH_2)_2CO$ — and is found in the urine of animals.

*Urine*  Diluted 2 to 1, urine makes an ideal compost heap activator. See Urea.

*Vermiculite*  A layered mineral, like mica, vermiculite breaks down eventually to clay particles (see Chapter 4). If heated, it expands and forms a very light, very absorbent material often added to potting compost for extra moisture retention.

*Water*  Chemists are constantly surprised by the fact that combining hydrogen and oxygen produces water. By their calculations it should produce almost anything *but* water! All living organisms are composed of a very high proportion of water, and water, along with carbon dioxide, is the main building material of all living matter. Water, like all other plant nutrients, can be added where it is lacking, and care must be taken when doing so. When watering plants in pots, it must be remembered that any additives or impurities in tap water accumulate in the compost and can eventually build up to harmful amounts — especially lime in hard water areas. Using rainwater, or water from a domestic filter, reduces the need to change potting compost.

If there has been no rain for a long time and soil is very dry, watering is pointless unless done very thoroughly: the water either runs off the surface or soaks into the top half-inch and no further, and then evaporates again very rapidly. If shallow watering is done frequently it can reduce a plant's drought resistance, since roots will tend to grow nearer the soil surface.

*Wettable powder*  The addition of a wetting agent to a powder pesticide facilitates its mixture with water.

*Wetting agent*  See Surfactant.

*Winter field beans*  See Green manures.

*Winter tares*  See Green manures.

*Winter wash*  See Tar-oil.

*Wood ash*  A useful source of potassium, wood ash is very alkaline, and best sprinkled on the compost heap.

*Worm compost*  See Chapter 6.

*Zinc*  Micronutrient for plants and animals, zinc is present in a variety of enzymes. It is poisonous in larger amounts but even where the level of zinc in soil is high, plants do not take it up in significant quantities (see Heavy metals).

# Insecticide table

The following is a table of insecticides registered for amateur use at the time of writing. It makes rather monotonous reading, and the most repeated phrases are 'broad spectrum' and 'toxic to bees and fish'. Few are systemic, and only one, gamma HCH, is a very persistent organochlorine. Most of the synthetic pyrethroids are very rapidly decomposed, but permethrin is fairly persistent.

Most of them — even the 'safe' derris — are quoted by one source or another as suspected carcinogens, mutagens or teratogens, and this has not been listed. The LD50 figure (see Chapter 5) has been included, but should not be taken as the most important fact about a pesticide. It must not be forgotten that the more toxic insecticides are only available to the gardener in safer formulations — either with a relatively small amount of active ingredient, or in a granular form. It is also true that some of the insecticides that are safest to humans are very effective insecticides — Bioresmethrin is reputedly 50 times as effective for killing houseflies as

natural pyrethrum, and also many times less poisonous to animals.

None of the broad-spectrum insecticides available to amateurs is particularly effective against two major glasshouse pests: glasshouse whitefly and red spider mite. These two are best controlled biologically (see Chapter 7).

All pesticides should be treated as irritants — of eye, lung and skin — even if they are not listed as such. Even soap stings your eyes, as every child finds out. If you do use pesticides, follow the instructions to the letter! Spray early in the morning or late in the afternoon, when few insects are active and the sun will not scorch plants. Do not spray plants in open flower.

Key OC = Organochlorine
OP = Organophosphate
C = Carbamate
SP = Synthetic pyrethroid
B = Biological or plant derivative
O = Other
~ = Roughly

# INSECTICIDES

| Common Name | Type | Uses | Remarks | LD50 (mg per kg) |
|---|---|---|---|---|
| Allethrin | SP | Household insects. Rapid 'knock down'. | Contact/stomach poison. Similar in effect to pyrethrins, usually more effective, usually with piperonyl butoxide synergist. Poisonous to fish and bees. | 1,100 |
| Bacillus thuringiensis | B | Butterfly and moth caterpillars. Approved by organic standards. | Bacterium, biological action. Non poisonous. Usually with pyrethrins. | |
| Bendiocarb | C | Broad spectrum. Commercially granular formulation for soil pests, but also as ant powder. | Highly hazardous contact + stomach poison. Very toxic to bees, fish, wild life. | 34-64 |
| Borax | O | Ants. | Also persistent herbicide (2 years). | |
| Bioresmethrin | SP | Broad spectrum. Rapid 'knock down'. | Contact + stomach poison. Very toxic to bees and fish. | 7,000 |
| Bromophos | OP | Broad spectrum. Soil pests. | Contact + stomach poison. Persists $\sim$ 10 days. Toxic to bees. | 3,750 |
| Carbaryl | C | Broad spectrum. Soil pests + worms. | Contact, stomach + systemic. Toxic to bees. Medium persistence. | 850 |
| Chlorpyrifos | OP | Broad spectrum. Soil pests. | Contact, stomach, vapour. Persists $\sim$ 4 months. Toxic to bees and fish. | 140 |
| Derris | | See Rotenone. | | |

*continued overleaf*

| Common Name | Type | uses | Remarks | LD50 (mg per kg) |
|---|---|---|---|---|
| Diazinon | OP | Broad spectrum. Soil pests. | Non-systemic. Very toxic to birds, bees, fish. | 300 |
| Dichlorvos | OP | Broad spectrum. Fly killer. | Contact, stomach, fumigant. Very toxic to bees, also fish, birds, Non-persistent. | 60 |
| Dimethoate | OP | Broad spectrum. | Systemic + contact. Very toxic to bees, fish, wild life. Persists ~ 10 days. | 200-300 |
| Fatty acids (soap) | O | Aphids, scale, mites, whitefly. Approved by organic standards. | Non toxic, non persistent. May harm plants. | |
| Fenitrothion | OP | Broad spectrum esp. caterpillars and sawfly larvae. | Contact poison. Toxic to bees, fish and wild life. | 250-800 |
| Gamma HCH | OC | Broad spectrum. | Stomach, contact + fumigant. Very persistent (3-12 months, or more). | 90 |
| Heptenophos | OP | Aphids, scale. | Systemic, short persistence. Toxic to bees, fish, wild life. | 100 |
| Lindane = gamma HCH | | | | |
| Malathion | | Broad spectrum. | Contact + stomach poison, low toxicity to mammals, but toxic to bees + fish. Medium persistence. | 2,800 |
| Permethrin | SP | Broad spectrum. | Contact + stomach poison. Toxic to bees, very toxic to fish. Persists 2—4 months. | varies with proportions of isomers 400-4,000 |

| Common Name | Type | Uses | Remarks | LD50 (mg per kg) |
|---|---|---|---|---|
| Phenothrin | SP | Household insects, Rapid 'knock down'. | Contact + stomach poison. Very poisonous to fish. | 10,000 |
| Piperonyl butoxide | O | Synergist for pyrethrin and pyrethroids. | Increases insecticidal effect without increasing toxicity to mammals. | 7,500 |
| Phoxim | OP | Broad spectrum. Soil pests. | Low mammalian toxicity but very toxic to bees and fish. | 2,000 |
| Pirimicarb | C | Selective aphicide. Effective against strains resistant to OPs. | Poisonous to man and wildlife, but safe to insects other than aphids. Non-fungicidal, non-acaricidal; used in IPM schemes. | 150 |
| Pirimiphos methyl | OP | Broad spectrum. Insects and mites. | Contact + fumigant. Toxic to bees and fish. Medium persistence. | 2,000 |
| Pyrethrum (pyrethrins) | B | Broad spectrum. Approved by organic standards. Rapid 'knock down'. | Contact poison, flower extract containing 6 different insecticides in varying proportions. Unstable in light and air. Toxic to bees and fish. Usually with piperonyl butoxide. | 300-900 |
| Quassia | B | Some effect against aphids, sawfly, caterpillars. Also cat and dog repellant. | Very low toxicity. Harmless to ladybirds, bees. Works partly as deterrent. Bitter taste may taint leaf crops for a week. | |
| Resmethrin | SP | Broad spectrum, esp. flies and wasps. Rapid 'knock down'. | Contact poison. Toxic to bees and fish. Non-persistent. | 2,500 |

*continued overleaf*

| Common Name | Type | Uses | Remarks | LD50 (mg per kg) |
|---|---|---|---|---|
| Rotenone (Derris) | B | Broad spectrum. | Contact poison. Short to medium persistence. From root of Derris elliptica. Toxic to bees, very toxic to fish. | 50-500 |
| Tar oil | O | Winter wash on fruit trees. | Toxic to eggs of many insect species. Very phytotoxic, also kills moss and lichen. Low toxicity to man, may cause dermatitis. | |
| Tetramethrin | SP | Broad spectrum, esp. flies and wasps. | Very low mammalian toxicity but toxic to fish and bees. Used with piperonyl butoxide. | 5,000 |

# *Fungicide table*

The table of fungicides, like that of insecticides, shows the predominance of broad-spectrum substances. It is the systemic ones, particularly benomyl, carbendazim, thiophanate-methyl, and thiabendazole, that have encountered resistance problems. If you are going to use them on a regular basis, they should be alternated with non-systemic fungicides.

Very few modern fungicides are highly toxic to mammals, but the old-fashioned, inorganic ones are more so, especially mercury, and they tend also to be more toxic to plants. They are nearly all suspected by someone of being carcinogenic, mutagenic or teratogenic, so this is not mentioned with the exception of benomyl, carbendazim, thiophanate methyl and thiabendazole, which work specifically as mutagens.

Treat all fungicides as irritants, even if they are not.

## FUNGICIDES

| Common Name | Uses | Remarks | LD50 (mg per kg) |
|---|---|---|---|
| Benomyl | Broad spectrum. | Protective, eradicant, systemic, medium persistence. Resistance problems. Works as a mutagen. Kills worms, mites, fish. | 10,000 |
| Bordeaux mixture | See copper sulphate. | | |

*continued overleaf*

| Common Name | Uses | Remarks | LD50 (mg per kg) |
|---|---|---|---|
| Bupirimate | Specific for powdery mildews. Used in IPM schemes. | Systemic, protectant. | 4,000 |
| Captan | Broad spectrum. | Protectant, eradicant, non-systemic. | 9,000 |
| Carbendazim | Broad spectrum. | Systemic, protectant similar to *benomyl*. | 15,000 |
| Copper oxychloride | Broad spectrum. | Protectant. Less phytotoxic than copper sulphate. Toxic to fish. Long persistence. | 1,440 |
| Copper sulphate | Broad spectrum. Used by organic gardeners. | Combined with lime makes 'Bordeaux mixture'. With other bases makes Burgundy and Cheshunt compounds. Risk of phytotoxicity. Poisonous to fish, long persistence, residues accumulate, toxic to earth-worms. | 300 |
| Dinocap | Broad spectrum. | Non-systemic. Protectant. Kills mites. | 1,000 |
| Fenarimol | Powdery mildews and rose blackspot. | Protective, eradicant, systemic, also short persistence. Poisonous to fish. | 2,500 |
| Mancozeb | Broad spectrum. | Protective, non-systemic, medium persistence. | 8,000 |
| Mercurous chloride (calomel) | Use restricted to soil application for brassica club root and onion white rot. | Eradicant. Highly toxic to plants and animals. Highly persistent. | 210 |
| Propiconazole | Broad spectrum. | Systemic, protectant. Medium persistence. | 1,500 |
| Pyrazophos | Powdery mildew. Also insecticide and acaricide. | Systemic. Derived from OP insecticide. Toxic to bees, fish and wildlife. | 150 |

FUNGICIDE TABLE

| Common Name | Uses | Remarks | LD50 (mg per kg) |
|---|---|---|---|
| Sodium hydrogen carbonate (Bicarbonate of soda) | Some effect against botrytis and powdery mildew, esp. used with a 'sticker'. Approved by organic standards. | Safe, non-persistent. | |
| Sulphur | Broad spectrum, esp. powdery mildews. Approved by organic standards. | Protectant. Phytotoxic to some species. Medium persistence. Kills mites including predators. | *see Footnote (1) |
| Tecnazene | Commercial potato sprout inhibitor. Smoke formulation for botrytis in greenhouses. | Non-systemic. | *see Footnote (2) |
| Thiabendazole | Broad spectrum. | Systemic. Similar to *benomyl* originally human and veterinary medicine for worms. | 3,300 |
| Thiophanate-methyl | Broad spectrum. | Systemic. Similar to *benomyl*. | 7,500 |
| Thiram | Broad spectrum. | Protectant, non-systemic. Poisonous to fish. | 800 |
| Triforine | Broad spectrum. | Systemic, protectant, medium persistence. | 16,000 |

Footnote (1): Sulphur is generally quoted as being of 'low mammalian toxicity'. The lowest fatal dose recorded was 500 mg/kg.

Footnote (2): Tecnazene is generally quoted as being of 'low mammalian toxicity'. One source put the LD50 oral rate at 250mg/kg.

# *Herbicide table*

Y ou may notice a large number of hormone-type lawn weedkillers. Two or three are usually combined since each has slightly better or worse control over different weeds.

Many of the remainder are marketed for the amateur as path weedkillers. In commercial practice, the varying efficacy of different herbicides for different weeds, and the varying resistance of various crops can be manipulated so that there is a weedkiller for almost every occasion. Whatever the pros and cons of weedkillers *per se*, it would be foolish for the amateur to use them among crops or valued ornamental plants without very precise knowledge of their effects.

Very few are acutely toxic to mammals but, as with insecticides and fungicides, most of them are quoted by some authority as carcinogens, teratogens or mutagens. Treat them all as irritants, just in case.

## HERBICIDES

| Common Name | Uses | Remarks | LD50 (mg per kg) |
|---|---|---|---|
| Alloxydim sodium | Selective grass esp. couch. | Foliar acting. Post-emergence. | 2,300 |
| Amino-triazole (Amitrole) | Esp. grasses, effective most others. | Translocated. Soil and foliar acting. Toxic to fish. | 1,100 |
| Ammonium sulphamate | Non-selective, esp. woody plants and deep-rooted perennials. Tree stumps. | Becomes ammonium sulphate (fertilizer) in 3 weeks. Used by some organic gardeners. | 3,900 |

| Common Name | Uses | Remarks | LD50 (mg per kg) |
|---|---|---|---|
| Atrazine | Paths. | Translocated, soil acting + some foliar action. Chemically similar to simazine. Long persistence. Toxic to fish. | 2-3,000 |
| Benzolin | Specific against chickweed, cleavers and charlock, used with 2,4-D, Dicamba etc. for lawns. | Translocated, post emergence. Toxic to fish. | 4,800 |
| Chloroxuron | Germinating seedlings and annuals + moss killer. | Soil acting, non-persistent. Toxic to fish. | 3,000 |
| 2, 4-D | Selective against broad-leaved plants. Lawn weedkiller. | Translocated, hormone type. Persists ∼ 1 month. Toxic to fish. | 375 |
| Dalapon | Selective against grasses. | Foliar acting. Contact + translocated. Non-persistent in soil | 7,500 |
| Dicamba | Selective against broad-leaved plants. Lawn weedkiller. | Translocated, post emergence. Poisonous to fish. Non-persistent in soil. | 1,700 |
| Dichlorophen | Moss killer, also fungicide, bactericide. | Dangerous to fish. | 1,250 |
| Dichlorprop | Selective against broad-leaved plants. Lawn weedkiller. | Translocated, hormone type. Dangerous to fish. | 800 |
| Diquat | Non-selective. Paths, annual weeds. | Contact. Similar to *paraquat* but less toxic. | 230 |
| Diuron | Non-selective, annuals, weed seedlings. Used for paths, uncultivated ground. | Soil acting, long persistence (6m-lyr). Toxic to fish. | 3,400 |

*continued overleaf*

| Common Name | Uses | Remarks | *LD50*<br>*(mg per kg)* |
|---|---|---|---|
| Fenoprop | Broad-leaved weeds. Lawn weedkiller. | Translocated hormone type. Toxic to fish. | 650 |
| Ferrous sulphate | Moss killer. | Traditional ingredient of Lawn sand. | |
| Glyphosate | Non-selective, good for deep rooted perennials. | Systemic, non-residual, post emergent. Soil inactivated then breaks down within 3 months. | 5,600 |
| MCPA | Selective broad-leaved plants. Lawn weedkiller. | Translocated, hormone type. Toxic to fish. | 700 |
| Mecoprop | Similar to MCPA. | | 930 |
| Paraquat | Non-selective. Paths, annual weeds among shrubs. | Highly toxic. Soil inactivated, remains bound to soil particles a long time. | 25 (dog) |
| Propachlor | Annual weeds between some crops. | Residual. Persists ∼ 6 weeks. Pre- or post-emergence. Toxic to fish. | 1,800 |
| Simazine | Annual weeds or seedlings in established crops or fruit, or path weedkiller. | Pre-emergent. Residual. | 5,000 |
| Sodium chlorate | Non-selective. Uncultivated ground, paths. | Explosive, but contains fire depressant. Long persistence (6 months). May 'creep' into cultivated areas. | 1,200 |
| 2,4,5-T | Perennial weeds, esp. woody species. | Translocated hormone type. Toxic to fish and wild life, very persistent. Contains traces of dioxin. Still registered but not manufactured for amateur use. *Not* the same as 2,4-D. | 300-1,500 |
| 2,3,6-TBA | Lawn weedkiller. 'Touchstick' for resistant weeds. | Translocated hormone type. Persists in treated plants. | 1,500 |

# Miscellaneous Tables

## Growth regulators

| Common Name | Uses | Remarks | LD50 (mg per kg) |
|---|---|---|---|
| Dikegulac | Growth regulator for hedges. | Retards growth — sort of chemical substitute for shears. Will it do topiary? | 20,000-30,000 |
| Maleic hydrazide | Growth regulator for lawns. | Retards growth (inhibits cell division). Why not dig up the lawn and plant something you *like* to grow? | 5,000 |
| 1-napthyl-acetic acid | Hormone rooting powder. | Assists formation of roots on cuttings. Always combined with a fungicide. | 1,000-6,000 |
| 2-napthyl oxyacetic acid | Tomato setting spray. | Improves setting of tomatoes and other fruit. | 600 |
| 4-indiol-3-ylbutyric acid | Hormone rooting powder. | Assists formation of roots on cuttings. Always combined with fungicide. | |

# Molluscicides

| Common Name | Uses | Remarks | LD50 (mg per kg) |
|---|---|---|---|
| Aluminium sulphate | Kills slugs and snails. | 'Safe' alternative to two following: also less effective. Acidifies soil, may harm young foliage. Good for 'blueing' hydrangeas. | low toxicity |
| Metaldehyde | Kills slugs and snails. | Danger to pets and wildlife. Bait contains pet deterrent. Blue colour deters birds. Risk reduced if pellets placed in inaccessible places. Fairly short persistence. | 600-1,000 (dog) |
| Methiocarb | Kills slugs and snails. | More toxic, more persistent than metaldehyde. Effective insecticide, also kills worms. Deters birds. | 100 |

# Worm killers

| Common Name | Uses | Remarks | LD50 (mg per kg) |
|---|---|---|---|
| Carbaryl | Worm killer. | Chlordane has been withdrawn for amateur use, only carbaryl remains — also insecticide. It is unfortunate that anyone should want to kill worms: they are very beneficial creatures; their presence indicates a healthy soil. The *problem* is that other pesticides also kill worms. | 850 |

# Vertebrate control

| Common Name | Uses | Remarks | LD50 (mg per kg) |
|---|---|---|---|
| Brodifacoum | Mouse killer. | The dangers of these are | 0.27 |
| Bromadiolone | Mouse and rat killer. | obvious. What will kill mice | 1.1 |
| Coumatetralyl | Mouse and rat killer. | and rats will kill larger | 0.3 |
| Difenacoum | Mouse and rat killer. | animals if eaten in larger | 1.8 |
| Warfarin | Mouse killer. | quantities. | 1.0 |
| Copper sulphate<br>Aluminium ammonium sulphate<br>Naphthalene<br>Pepper<br>Quassia | Dog, cat and bird repellants | Generally ineffective. See fungicide table for copper sulphate; insecticide table for quassia. | |

# Pesticide products

There are nearly 3,000 registered pesticide products in this country, of which a small proportion are available to the amateur. Not all the registered products are still manufactured, but they still have a registration and they are still legally usable. For instance, 2,4,5-T is still registered for amateur use, but there is no longer any amateur product manufactured that contains it. All the products in the following list should be available, but it is a rapidly shifting market and it is quite likely that some chemicals and therefore products will be withdrawn at any time, and others revamped and renamed. The products listed have been selected for a variety of active ingredients, so that nearly all the approved active ingredients in the pesticide tables get a mention.

| Trade Name | Marketing company | Purpose | Chemical contents |
|---|---|---|---|
| Amcide | Battle Hayward & Bower Ltd | Herbicide | Ammonium Sulphamate |
| Bactospeine | Koppert (UK) Ltd | Insecticide | Bacillus Thuringiensis + Pyrethrins |
| Benlate | ICI PLC | Fungicide | Benomyl |
| BIO Cropsaver | P.B.I. Ltd | Insecticide | Malathion & pyrethrins |
| BIO Flydown | P.B.I. Ltd | Insecticide | Permethrin |
| BIO Long Last | P.B.I. Ltd | Insecticide | Dimethoate & permethrin |
| BIO Multirose | P.B.I. Ltd | Fungicide & Insecticide | Dinocap, permethrin, sulphur, Triforine |

## PESTICIDE PRODUCTS

| Trade Name | Marketing company | Purpose | Chemical contents |
|---|---|---|---|
| BIO Multiveg | P.B.I. Ltd | Fungicide & Insecticide | Carbendazin, copper oxychloride, permethrin sulphur. |
| Boots Multiveg | The Boots Co. PLC | Insecticide | Carbaryl + sodium tetraborate |
| Boots garden insect powder | The Boots Co. PLC | Insecticide | Carbaryl + rotenone |
| Boots garden insect spray | The Boots Co. PLC | Insecticide | Lindane + pyrethrins |
| Boots greenfly & blackfly killer | The Boots Co. PLC | Insecticide | Dimethoate |
| Boots Hormone rooting powder | The Boots Co. PLC | Fungicide/ Herbicide | 4-indol-3-ylbutyric acid + 1-Naphthylacetic acid + Thiram |
| Boots long-lasting weedkiller | The Boots Co. PLC | Herbicide | Amitrole + atrazine |
| Boots slug destroyer pellets | The Boots Co. PLC | Molluscicide | Metaldehyde |
| Boots total lawn treatment | The Boots Co. PLC | Herbicide | Benazolin + 2, 4-D + dicamba + dichlorophen + dichlorprop + mecoprop |
| Bordeaux Mixture | Synchemicals Ltd | Fungicide | Copper complex |
| Bordeaux Mixture | Battle Hayward & Bower Ltd | Fungicide | Copper sulphate + sodium hydrogen carbonate |
| Bug gun | ICI PLC | Insecticide | Pyrethrum |
| Cat off | Fieldspray Ltd | Vertebrate control | Quassia |
| Camco ant powder | Camco Ltd | Insecticide | Bendiocarb |

*continued overleaf*

| Trade Name | Marketing company | Purpose | Chemical contents |
|---|---|---|---|
| Cooper garden pet killers | Ashe Consumer Products Ltd | Insecticide | Bioresmethrin |
| Dog off | Fieldspray Ltd | Vertebrate control | Quassia |
| Fentro | Fisons PLC | Insecticide | Fenitrothion |
| Fertosan slug killer | Fertosan Products Ltd | Molluscicide | Aluminium sulphate |
| Fisons Lawncare Liquid | Fisons PLC | Herbicide | Dicamba + MCPA + mecoprop |
| Fisons New Evergreen 90 | Fisons PLC | Herbicide | Mecoprop + benazolin + MCPA |
| Fisons Path Weedkiller | Fisons PLC | Herbicide | Amitrole + MCPA + simazine |
| Floret Fast Knock down | Reckitt Household Products Ltd | Insecticide | Allethrin |
| Fungus Fighter | May & Baker (Rhone-Poulenc) | Fungicide | Thiophanate-Methyl |
| Greenhouse Smoke Disease Killer | May & Baker (Rhone-Poulenc) | Fungicide | Tecnazene |
| Hytrol | Agrichem Ltd | Herbicide | Amitrole + 2, 4-D + divron + simazine |
| ICI slug pellets | ICI PLC | Molluscicide | Metaldehyde |
| Kerispray | ICI | Insecticide | Pirimiphos-methyl + pyrethrins |
| Koppert De-moss | Koppert (UK) Ltd | Herbicide | Fatty acids |
| Mossgun | ICI | Herbicide | Chloroxuron, dichlorophen + ferrous sulphate |
| Murphy ant killer powder | Fisons PLC | Insecticide | Lindane |

| Trade Name | Marketing company | Purpose | Chemical contents |
|---|---|---|---|
| Murphy combined seed dressing | Fisons PLC | Insecticide/ fungicide | Captan & lindane |
| Murphy Covershield weed preventer | Fisons PLC | Herbicide | Propachlor |
| Murphy Derris Dust | Fisons PLC | Insecticide | Rotenone |
| Murphy Hormone Rooting powder | Fisons PLC | Fungicide/ herbicide | Captan + 1 naphthylacetic acid |
| Murphy Kil-Ant | Fisons PLC | Insecticide | Phoxim |
| Murphy Malathion Liquid | Fisons PLC | Insecticide | Malathion |
| Murphy Mole Smoke | Fisons PLC | Vertebrate control | Sulphur |
| Murphy Mortegg | Fisons PLC | Insecticide | Tar oils + phenols |
| Murphy Pathweed Killer | Fisons PLC | Herbicide | Amitrole + Atrazine |
| Murphy Rootguard | Fisons PLC | Insecticide | Diazinon |
| Murphy Sodium chlorate | Fisons PLC | Herbicide | Sodium chlorate |
| Murphy Super slugits | Fisons PLC | Molluscicide | Metaldehyde |
| Murphy systemic insecticide | Fisons PLC | Insecticide | Dimethoate |
| Murphy Tumbleblite | Fisons PLC | Fungicide | Propiconazole |
| Murphy Tumblebug | Fisons PLC | Insecticide | Heptenphos + permethrin |
| Murphy Tumbleweed | Fisons PLC | Herbicide | Glyphosate |

*continued overleaf*

| Trade Name | Marketing company | Purpose | Chemical contents |
|---|---|---|---|
| Murphy Zap-cap General Insecticide | Fisons PLC | Insecticide | Permethrin |
| Murphy Zap-cap Comb. insecticide/ fungicide | Fisons PLC | Insecticide | Fenarimol + Permethrin |
| Nimrod T | ICI | Fungicide | Bupirimate + triforine |
| Nippon ant & crawling insect powder | Synchemicals Ltd | Insecticide | Tetramethrin + permethrin |
| Nobble garden pack | Fieldpray Ltd | Miscellaneous | Aluminium ammonium sulphate + copper sulphate + sodium tetraborate |
| Pathclear | ICI | Herbicide | Amitrole + diquate + paraquat + simazine |
| PBI Autumn & Winter Toplawn | PBI | Miscellaneous & wormkiller | Carbaryl |
| PBI Boltac Grease Bands | PBI | Insecticide | Grease |
| PBI Bromophos | PBI | Insecticide | Bromophos |
| PBI Calomel Dust | PBI | Fungicide | Mercurous chloride |
| PBI Cheshunt Compound | PBI | Fungicide | Copper sulphate + ammonium carbonate |
| PBI Dithane 945 | PBI | Fungicide | Mancozeb |
| PBI Hexyl | PBI | Insecticide/ fungicide | Lindane + rotenone + thiram |
| PBI Slug mini pellets | PBI | Molluscicide | Metaldehyde |
| PBI slug-guard | PBI | Molluscicide | Methiocarb |

| Trade Name | Marketing company | Purpose | Chemical contents |
|---|---|---|---|
| Phostrogen Safer's Ready-to-use Fruit and Vegetable insecticide | Phostrogen Ltd | Insecticide | Fatty acids |
| Phostrogen Safer's Ready-to-use Garden fungicide | Phostrogen Ltd | Fungicide | Sulphur |
| Roseclear | ICI | Fungicide/ insecticide | Pirimicarb + bupirimate + triforine |
| Safer's Natural Garden Fungicide | Koppert UK Ltd | Fungicide | Sulphur |
| Savona | Koppert UK Ltd | Insecticide | Fatty acids |
| Secto Aphid Killer | Secto Co. Ltd | Insecticide | Dichlorvos + lindane tetramethrin |
| Secto Derris Dust | Secto Co. Ltd | Insecticide | Rotenone |
| Secto Rose and Flower spray | Secto Co. Ltd | Fungicide/ insecticide | Dimethoate + lindane + thiram |
| Sectovap | Secto Co. Ltd | Insecticide | Dichlorvos |
| Secto Vegetable Insect Powder | Secto Co. Ltd | Insecticide | Diazinon + lindane |
| Secto wasp killer powder | Secto Co. Ltd | Insecticide | Carbaryl + pyrethrins |
| Stay off | Synchemicals Ltd | Miscellaneous | Aluminium ammonium sulphate |
| Sybol 2 Aerosol | ICI | Insecticide | Permethrin |
| Sybol 2 | ICI | Insecticide | Pirimiphos-methyl |
| Synchemicals Couch and Grass killer | Synchemicals Ltd | Herbicide | Dalapon |

*continued overleaf*

HOW GREEN IS YOUR GARDEN?

| Trade Name | Marketing company | Purpose | Chemical contents |
|---|---|---|---|
| Synchemicals New 4-50 Lawn Weedspray | Synchemicals Ltd | Herbicide | 2, 4-D + fenoprop |
| Synchemicals Tomato setting spray | Synchemicals Ltd | Herbicide | 2-Naphthyloxyacetic acid |
| Synchemicals New Formulation Brushwood Killer | Synchemicals Ltd | Herbicide | 2, 4-D Dicamba + mecoprop |
| Touchweeder | Thomas Elliot Ltd | Herbicide | 2, 4-D + 2, 3, 6-TBA |
| Weedol | ICI | Herbicide | Diquat + paraquat |
| Weedout | May & Baker/ (Rhone-Poulenc) | Herbicide | Alloxydim-sodium |

# Organic product table

There is no legal definition of 'organic'. There are various organic standards, the most stringent of which is the Soil Association's, and anything can be sold as 'organic'. Fertilizers like blood, fish and bonemeal are produced by many firms and are available in garden centres. Derris and pyrethrum, copper sulphate, and sulphur are produced by the big agrochemical firms and are also easily available, but most have to be acquired by mail order from specialist suppliers. Some products can be bought direct from manufacturers or other suppliers such as Cumulus Organics and Chase Organics, but the HDRA — the main organic gardening organization in Britain — supplies most of the products listed. See the list of addresses. Major seed firm catalogues have now started promoting a few organic products.

## ORGANIC PRODUCTS

| Product name | Manufacturer or supplier | Remarks |
|---|---|---|
| Aeroxon Flying Insect Traps | HDRA Suffolk Herbs | Non-toxic 'sticky' traps for greenhouse control control of whiteflies, aphids etc. |
| Agryl P | HDRA | Polypropylene fibre cloth for use over vegetables: keeps out flying insects, lets in water or light. |
| Bactospeine | Koppert UK Suffolk Herbs | Bacillus thuringiensis, bacterial spray to kill caterpillars. |

*continued overleaf*

| Product name | Manufacturer or supplier | Remarks |
|---|---|---|
| Biological emhols: phytoseuilis persimilis | HDRA HDRA | Predator of glasshouse red spider mite. |
| Encarsia formosa | HDRA | Predator of glasshouse whitefly. |
| Bacillus thuringiensis | HDRA | See 'Bactospeine'. |
| Binab T pellets | HDRA | Trichoderma fungus prevents infection of fruit trees by silver leaf disease fungus. |
| Comfrey | HDRA Suffolk Herbs | 'Bocking 14' is the variety grown as a perennial to supply compost material or to make liquid feed. |
| Cowpact | Cowpact products | Compressed composted compacts. |
| Cowpost | Cowpact products Suffolk Herbs | Mixture of peat and cow manure. Multi-purpose compost, HDRA recommended. |
| Farmura Liquid organic fertilizer | CUMULUS organics Suffolk Herbs | Made from farmyard manure |
| Fertosan slug killer | Fertosan Suffolk Herbs | Contains aluminium sulphate. |
| Fertosan Compost Maker | Fertosan | A culture of micro-organisms to accelerate the composting process. |
| Fertilizers, organic Bloodfish & bonemeal Bonemeal Calcified seaweed Dolomite Gypsum Hoof & Horn Rock phosphate Rock potash Seaweed meal | HDRA Suffolk Herbs | See A to Z. |
| Forestbark | ICI | A bark product for paths and mulching trees and shrubs. Available from garden centres. |

| Product name | Manufacturer or supplier | Remarks |
|---|---|---|
| Fyba cabbage collars | | Prevent cabbage root fly from reaching roots. Available from garden centres. Easy to make your own, and cheaper. |
| Garden Mulch | Cowpact Products | A mixture of shredded bark leaves and woodchips, for paths and mulching trees and shrubs. |
| Green manures various species | HDRA Suffolk Herbs | See list of 'substances' on page 73. |
| Kemp shredder/ chipper | Globe Garden Services | Chips wood waste for your own path or shrub mulch, or shreds material for the compost heap. |
| Kemp compost tumbler | Globe Garden Services | Useful if you have a large supply of compost material. |
| Koppert original fungicide | Koppert UK | Contains sulphur. |
| Maxicrop natural seaweed extract | Stimgro | Concentrated liquid seaweed for liquid feed or foliar spray. Other Maxicrop products contain 'artificial' ingredients, so purists beware. See Seaweed in the A to Z. |
| Nobble slug killer | Fieldspray Ltd | Similar to 'Fertosan', contains potassium permanganate and copper sulphate as well as aluminium sulphate. Available from garden centres. |
| PBI Greasebands | PBI | For fruit tree protection in winter. Available from garden centres. |
| Papronet | HDRA | Fine mesh polythene for greenhouse shading, carrot-fly barriers, etc. |
| Pesticides various: Derris, pyrethrim Quassia, soft soap Bordeaux mixture | HDRA CHASE organics CUMULUS organics | See insecticides and fungicides lists. |

*continued overleaf*

| Product name | Manufacturer or supplier | Remarks |
|---|---|---|
| Phostrogen — Safers Insecticidal soap | Phostrogen Suffolk Herbs | Contains fatty acids, various strengths available. Ready mixed in spray guns. Expensive. |
| Phostrogen Safers Natural Garden fungicide | Phostrogen Suffolk Herbs | Contains sulphur. Ready mixed in spray gun. Expensive. |
| QR Compost Activator | HDRA Suffolk Herbs | A herbal mixture to accelerate compost making. |
| Savona insecticidal soap | Koppert UK Suffolk Herbs | Contains fatty acids. |
| Seeds: various untreated organically grown wild flower herb old varieties | HDRA Suffolk Herbs E.W. King CHASE organics CUMULUS organics | |
| SM3 seaweed extract | HDRA Suffolk Herbs | Seaweed liquid feed. Soil Association (SA) approved. |
| Stimgro | Stimgro | Cow manure and peat — a multi-purpose compost. Available in garden centres. |
| Super Natural organic compost | HDRA | Used as a general fertilizer, or mixed with peat to make your own potting or seed compost. SA approved. |
| Trappit Codling Moth trap | HDRA | Contains a 'pheromone' lure for male moths, leaving females unfertilized. |
| Turning worms compost | Turning Worms | Peat, moss, sand, seaweed fish and bonemeal worked and blended by brandling worms. (Eisenia foetida). SA approved (see worm compost). |
| Worms | Turning Worms | If you can't find any brandling worms in your compost heap, HDRA have them. |

# Addresses

The British Agrochemicals Association
4 Lincoln Court
Lincoln Road
Peterborough PE1 2RP.
Tel. (0733) 49225.

The BAA represents the bigger manufacturers and formulators of pesticides in Britain. The *Directory of Garden Chemicals* is available from them and lists many of the amateur products available from the following firms:

Agrichem Ltd
First Drove
Fengate
Peterborough PE1 5BJ.

The Boots Company PLC
Nottingham NG2 3AA.

Fisons PLC
(includes Murphy Home & Garden Products) Horticulture Division
Paper Mill Lane
Bramford
Ipswich IP8 4BZ.

ICI Garden Products
Woolmead House East
Woolmead Walk
Farnham
Surrey GU9 7UB.

Pan Britannica (PBI)
Britannica House
Waltham Cross
Herts EN8 7DY.

Rhone-Poulenc
(May & Baker Garden)
Regents House
Hubert Road
Brentwood
Essex CM14 4TZ.

Synchemicals Ltd
44/45 Grange Walk
London SE1 3EN.

The Henry Doubleday Research Association
National Centre for Organic Gardening
Ryton-on-Dunsmore
Coventry CV8 3LG.
Tel. (0203) 303517

The HDRA is Britain's largest organic gardening organization. For £12 a year you get four excellent newsletters full of interesting information and a 'pull out' section of organic techniques, an annual catalogue of seeds, fertilizers, pesticides, books, etc. Whether you consider yourself organic or not, it is a very useful organization. You can visit their gardens, where all manner of organic methods are tried and tested. They have a 'seed bank' of rare or threatened species, and they also support various research programmes, including one to find trees that will grow in desert lands. They supply a large range of organic products, including most of those supplied by the following firms.

Chase Organics (GB) Ltd
Coombelands House
Coombelands Lane
Addlestone
Weybridge KT15 1HY.
Tel. (0932) 858511

Cumulus Organics & Conservation Ltd
Two Mile Lane
Highnam
Gloucester GL2 8DW.
Tel. (0452) 305814

E.W. King & Co. Ltd
Monks Farm
Pantlings Lane
Coggeshall Road
Kelvedon
Essex CO5 9PG.
Tel. (0376) 7000

Suffolk Herbs Ltd
Sawyers Farm
Little Cornard

Sudbury
Suffolk CO10 0NY.
Tel. (0787) 227247

Turning Worms
Perthi Yard
Llanrhystud
Dyfed SY23 5EH.
Tel. (09746) 240

*Chase Organics* and *Cumulus Organics* supply a wide range of organic products, and also Amcide, the herbicide which, though not 'organic', is used by many organic gardeners.

*Suffolk Herbs* sells all manner of seeds: herbs, wild flowers, green manures, 'conservation mixtures' and many more, as well as other organic products.

*E.W. King* specialize in undressed seed.

*Turning Worms* does not operate by mail order; products are available from HDRA, but they will give further advice on worm compost.

Chempak Products
Dept. 3
Geddings Road
Hoddesdon
Hertfordshire EN11 0LR.

Not an organic supplier. They have a large list of fertilizers, including slow-release types.

# Index